Brain Function
and
Reading Disabilities

Brain Function and Reading Disabilities

edited by

Lester Tarnopol, Sc.D.

Faculties of Engineering, Psychology, and Mathematics
City College of San Francisco

and

Muriel Tarnopol, M.A.

Assistant Professor
Departments of Counseling and Guidance, and Special Education
San Francisco State University

University Park Press
Baltimore·London·Tokyo

UNIVERSITY PARK PRESS
International Publishers in Science and Medicine
Chamber of Commerce Building
Baltimore, Maryland 21202

Typeset by Action Comp Co., Inc.
Manufactured in the United States of America by Universal Lithographers, Inc., and the Optic Bindery Incorporated.

Library of Congress Cataloging in Publication Data
Main entry under title:

Brain function and reading disabilities.

   Includes index.
   1. Reading disability—Addresses, essays, lectures.
2. Neuropsychology—Addresses, essays, lectures.
3. Brain—Addresses, essays, lectures. I. Tarnopol,
Lester. II. Tarnopol, Muriel. [DNLM: 1. Dyslexia.
2. Brain—Physiology. 3. Learning disorders. WL340
B816]
LB1050.5.B69   428'.4   77-6300
ISBN 0-8391-1130-4

Contents

Contributors

Dirk J. Bakker, Ph.D.
Head, Department of Developmental and Educational Neuropsychology, Pedagogical Institute, Koningslaan 22, Amsterdam (Z), The Netherlands

Jan de Wit, Ph.D.
Director, Pedagogical Institute, Koningslaan 22, Amsterdam (Z), and Professor of Clinical Child Psychology, Free University of Amsterdam, The Netherlands

James Evans, Ph.D.
Professor of Psychology, University of South Carolina, Columbia, South Carolina

Lawrence C. Hartlage, Ph.D.
Associate Professor of Neurology and Pediatrics, Medical College of Georgia, Augusta, Georgia

Patricia L. Hartlage, M.D.
Assistant Professor of Neurology and Pediatrics, Medical College of Georgia, Augusta, Georgia

Edmond Henry Keir, B.A., T.T.C.T.D., M.A.Ps.S., M.Aud.S.A.
Audiologist, Royal Children's Hospital, Melbourne, Australia

Aleksandr Romanovich Luria, Ph.D.
Professor Emeritus, Psychology Department, University of Moscow, and Institute of Defectology, and Member, Academy of Pedagogical Sciences, Moscow, U.S.S.R.

Lester Tarnopol, Sc.D.
Faculties of Engineering, Psychology, and Mathematics, City College of San Francisco, San Francisco, California

Muriel Tarnopol, M.A.
Assistant Professor, Departments of Counseling and Guidance, and Special Education, San Francisco State University, San Francisco, California

Acknowledgments

The editors gratefully acknowledge the assistance of everyone who contributed to this volume. We are especially grateful to Dr. A. R. Luria for permission to publish his chapter, "Cerebral Organization of Conscious Acts," which was originally given as a lecture to the XIX International Congress of Psychology in London in 1969.

We wish to thank Little, Brown and Company for permission to reproduce seven figures from *Learning Disorders in Children: Diagnosis, Medication, Education.*

We also wish to thank University Park Press for permission to reproduce two figures from *Reading Disabilities—An International Perspective.*

Preface

The major purpose of *Brain Function and Reading Disabilities*[1] is to prepare a small book on brain function that would prove useful as an auxiliary text in a course such as "Teaching the Learning Handicapped," or "Introduction to Learning Disabilities." Because texts covering the major subject matter are being used in these courses and only part of each course is devoted to brain function, a brief introductory text is needed for this part of these courses. Several professors of education have asked for this type of text, so it was prepared to fit their needs. The book may also be used in psychology, speech, hearing and language courses and others.

All of the chapters except Dr. A. A. Luria's were prepared especially for this volume and have not been published elsewhere.

---

[1] This is the fourth book edited in a series on reading and learning disabilities. It was necessary to edit a series of books because the subject is too vast for coverage in a single volume. The other books in this series are *Learning Disabilities: Introduction to Educational and Medical Management,* C C Thomas, 1969 (Spanish edition, La Prensa Medica Mexicana; Japanese edition, Nihon Bunka Kagaku-sha, Tokyo); *Learning Disorders in Children: Diagnosis, Medication, Education,* Little, Brown and Company, 1971 (Italian edition, Armando Armando Editore, Rome; Portuguese edition, Edart Livraria Editora, Sao Paulo; Russian edition, Moscow); and *Reading Disabilities: An International Perspective,* University Park Press, 1976.

To the dedicated teachers, psychologists, speech, hearing, and language therapists, physicians, nurses, and others who are helping children with learning disabilities.

Brain Function
and
Reading Disabilities

Chapter 1

Introduction to Neuropsychology

*Lester Tarnopol
and
Muriel Tarnopol*

Learning is a biological phenomenon. The abilities to use language and to read, write, spell, and solve mathematical problems are learned phenomena that result from biochemical functions within the nervous system. The central nervous system (CNS), especially those portions of the human brain committed to the higher functions, is the primary mediator of learning abilities. Conversely, any dysfunction in these areas of the brain disturbs the learning process. The relationships between various parts of the brain and learning have been investigated in sufficient detail to make this type of information useful to teachers, psychologists, speech therapists, physicians, and others interested in the diagnosis and remediation of people with learning disabilities.

There are, of course, limitations to such knowledge at present. We recognize that specific applications are only possible in a limited number of cases. However, some of the cases where brain function theory has been directly applied to practice have been most dramatic. Luria (1972) cites such an example in the case of Zasetsky, a soldier, who had a traumatic bullet wound in the left brain hemisphere where the temporal, parietal, and occipital lobes meet (Figure 1).

1

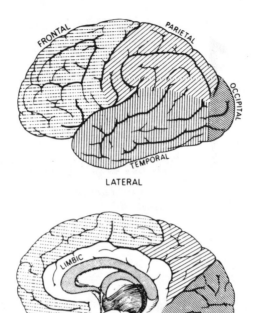

LATERAL

MEDIAL

Figure 1. Human cerebral hemisphere, lateral and medial views, showing lobes of the brain. (Reprinted with permission from Calanchini and Trout, 1971.)

Zasetsky had forgotten how to hold a pencil, how to form letters, and how to spell. When he tried to write, all he could do was "draw some crooked lines." Zasetsky later wrote in his diary, "It looked something like the scribbling of a child who still hasn't learnt the alphabet. It seemed funny, but also weird that I'd done that."

In attempting to relearn how to write, Zasetsky proceeded as a child would, trying to visualize each letter as he formed it. This proved to be a most difficult task because he had great trouble remembering the shapes of letters.

Luria states, "For adults, writing is an automatic skill, a series of built-in movements which I call 'kinetic melodies.' Hence, why shouldn't he try to use what skills he still had? His injury, after all, had damaged his capacity to see and orient himself spatially, but had not affected his kinetic-motor function." It was therefore suggested to Zasetsky that he try writing rapidly and automatically instead of letter by letter. At first, Zasetsky could not understand this curious suggestion, but after he tried it, he discovered he could write fairly well if he wrote spontaneously. This discovery made it possible for Zasetsky to write his biography, which is why we know of his struggle to regain his lost memory and "to recover a life I lost when I was wounded and became ill."

Can this type of reasoning be applied to assist children with learning disabilities who may not have had traumatic brain injuries? Numerous instances of successful applications of brain function to learning have been recorded. An especially interesting case comes from the Pacific Medical Center in San Francisco, a learning disabilities clinic, where neurological and psychometric examinations are done on all children. In the case of Paul, a young patient, the usual remedial methods were completely ineffective in teaching him to read. He got nowhere.

At Paul's case conference, it was noted that he had an unusually severe visual-perceptual disability that extended to his visual-motor integration. His auditory and auditory-motor functions, on the other hand, were intact and strong. One might say that his areas of brain dysfunction were similar to Zasetsky's. However, Zasetsky was an adult who had previously learned to read and write, while Paul was a child who was just in the process of trying to learn. Therefore, in Paul's case automatic writing could not be used. The case conferees concluded that it would be necessary to blindfold Paul in order to teach him to read! This method worked extremely well. They prescribed a "learning to read through writing" method. First, he was taught to write and spell while blindfolded, to prevent his dysfunctioning visual perceptions from interfering, as he used his intact auditory-kinesthetic modalities. When this learning was secure, the blindfold was removed and visual reading was introduced, tying it to his previous learning. In this way, Paul learned to write, spell, and read quite well.

LEARNING DISABILITIES DEFINED

The United States Office of Education defined *specific learning disabilities* in 1970. Children with specific learning disabilities were defined as "Those children who have a disorder in one or more of the basic psychological processes involved in understanding or in using language, spoken or written, which disorder may manifest itself in imperfect ability to listen, think, speak, read, write, spell, or do mathematical calculations. Such disorders include such conditions as perceptual handicaps, brain injury, minimal brain dysfunction, dyslexia, and developmental aphasia. Such term does not include children who have learning problems which are primarily the result of visual, hearing, or motor handicaps, of mental retardation, or of environmental disadvantage."

The term *general learning disabilities* has been similarly defined, except that it refers to children who are mentally retarded. These definitions are in agreement with those proposed and accepted by the Council for Exceptional Children. The concept of exceptional children refers to children outside the "normal range" and includes both the gifted and the retarded as well as all types of handicapped children.

BRAIN ORGANIZATION AND FUNCTION

Originally, it was believed that each different form of behavior must be regulated by a specific group of brain cells. However, Lashley (1929) performed a classic series of experiments on rats which demostrated that different parts of the brain were equipotential for complex behavioral functions, provided the specific known localized areas for motor, visual, and auditory processes remained intact. Essentially, he found that the rat's loss of ability to traverse a maze was dependent on the amount of brain removed rather than on the specific parts of the brain removed. This led to the holistic theory, which emphasizes how the brain functions as a whole.

A more cohesive concept of brain function grew out of a synthesis of these two earlier theories (Calanchini and Trout, 1971). The subtle anatomical differences among various areas of the cortex and their connections to different groups of receptors (visual, sensory, auditory, motor, etc.) tend to justify the concept that there may be as many different functional units as there are anatomical units. These individual brain cells and groups of cells process the information from specific receptors and stimuli. They may be activated or inhibited by these specific stimuli. On the other hand, complex functions, such as learning language, reading, writing, and thinking, are handled by many units in different parts of the brain working together. Various parts of the brain work together temporarily to perform some integrated behavior. Later, these same brain units may coordinate to perform a different behavior.

Luria (1966) summarized this concept: "The material basis of the higher nervous processes is the brain as a whole, but (at the same time) the brain is a highly differentiated system whose parts are responsible for different aspects of the unified whole." Luria suggested a relationship between brain function and behavior called "dynamic localization of cortical functions." Any specific behavior is the result of sequences of activities in groups of brain cells temporarily acting together. If one of these units dysfunctions, the resulting behavioral performances will be impaired. For example, in the cases of both Zasetsky and Paul, severe deficits in visual perception affected a number of related behaviors such as reading, writing, spelling, mathematics, and so forth.

Brain Function and Learning Disabilities

The causes of learning problems in nonretarded persons may include one or more of the following well known possibilities, adapted from a listing in Tarnopol and Tarnopol (1976).

1. Deficiencies in educational stimulation during the first 6 years
2. Excessive school absences

3. Changing schools too often
4. Lack of environmental motivators
5. Defects in teaching
6. Chronic illness or malnourishment
7. Severe hearing or vision loss
8. Genetic-specific learning disabilities
9. Brain damage

Neurological learning disabilities in children may result from many causes. These include genetic differences, maturational lags, chemical imbalances, brain injuries, and general or specific reduced functioning based on the normal variations in the various sensory learning modalities.

Research has indicated that at least one-third of the cases of specific learning disabilities have a genetic origin. It is not unusual to find reading, spelling, and/or mathematics disabilities running in families. Maturational lags may also be of genetic origin. Such lags prevent children from efficiently learning those things for which they are not sufficiently developmentally mature. These children will ordinarily be able to catch up academically if they do not develop severe emotional problems as the result of too much frustration connected with learning. Chemical imbalances may affect brain function adversely and consequently learning. Brain injuries clearly may have a similiar effect.

Dysfunction in any given area of the brain can disturb the learning functions in one or more modalities without affecting others. This is seen in the very large number of different types of learning disabilities that may occur in children. Problems may arise in any one or more of the sensory learning modalities within the visual, auditory, and somesthetic systems.

Some children can learn the sounds of letters but are unable to connect the visual images with these sounds. Other children may be able to learn visually but be unable to reproduce what they see in writing. Still others may be capable of understanding information received by the various senses but may be unable to retrieve this information to tell what they know.

Sometimes information received through one sensory channel interferes with the functioning of a different sensory modality. Such children are said to become overloaded. When this happens, they tend to disintegrate behaviorally. For example, young children may break down and cry.

According to Calanchini and Trout (1971), understanding brain anatomy and physiology and their relationships to brain function should permit a better comprehension of a child's learning disability, regardless of its etiology. They continue, "Even at this early stage of knowledge it is possible to relate the neurology of learning to diagnostic appraisal and educational remediation of children with neurological learning disabilities. What is known about the brain and learning can be incorporated in the selection of a diagnostic test battery, in outlining guidelines for the interpretation of test data and behavior, and in determining the selection of remediation materials and techniques."

CORTICAL ORGANIZATION OF THE BRAIN

The *cerebral cortex* is the outer layer of nerve cells covering the two hemispheres of the brain. All conscious activity appears to be controlled by the cerebral cortex. The cortex appears slightly pink *in situ* because of the blood supply. However, in the preserved state it appears gray, hence the common term "gray matter."

The human cortex is extremely wrinkled, convoluted, and fissured. These convolutions and fissures vastly increase the total usable area of the cortex. Of approximately 12 billion neurons in the human brain, 9 billion are in the cerebral cortex. In general, the amount of cortex in proportion to the total brain increases as organisms ascend the phylogentic scale.

Each hemisphere of the brain (left and right) is divided into four lobes: frontal, temporal, parietal, and occipital (Figure 1). The primary sensory processes are represented on the cerebral cortex, each in its own receptive area. On the cytoarchitectural map of the cortex, area 17 (occipital lobe) is the primary visual area (Figure 2). These cells respond to simple visual stimuli such as lines and edges. Areas 18 and 19 are higher order visual (secondary association) areas whose neurons are excited by more complex forms such as angles and rectangles. Perception of forms is dependent upon the way in which the visual areas of the brain are wired. One tends to see certain basic shapes very clearly because the neurons in the visual cortex respond selectively to these angles and shapes. Confused perceptions of visual forms and shapes may be related to either genetic wiring differences or to traumatic disturbances of the nerve cells.

In the temporal lobes, areas 41 and 42 receive auditory input. Each ear is connected to both the left and right hemispheres. However, it has been found that the left ear usually has its primary projection in the right hemisphere, while the right ear generally has its primary projection on the left hemisphere. Areas 41, 42, and 22 constitute the auditory analyzer. Area 41 contains the central or primary auditory field, while areas 42 and 22 are association areas, responsible for further and more complex analysis and synthesis of the information heard.

Areas 1, 2, and 3 (parietal lobe) constitute the primary, body-sense area; the cutaneous-kinesthetic (somesthetic) analyzer. These areas are backed up by the association zones for somesthesis, areas 5 and 7, which are responsible for further and more complex analysis and synthesis of tactile-kinesthetic information. Areas 1, 2, and 3 constitute the sensory strip behind the central fissure (fissure of Rolando) separating the frontal from the parietal lobe. This body-sense area detects pain, touch, cold, heat, and the feeling of body movement. The lower extremities on the right side of the body are represented high on the sensory strip of the left hemisphere, while the upper body parts appear on the lower areas of this strip (Figure 3). Similarly, the left side of the body is represented on the sensory strip of the right hemisphere.

The primary motor strip is area 4, located in front of the central fissure at the rear of the frontal lobe. The frontal lobe of the brain controls, among other things, the formulation and

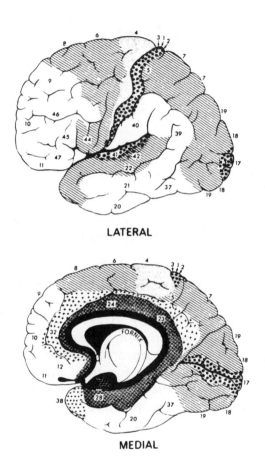

Figure 2. Cytoarchitectural map of human cerebral cortex. Areas with large dots, primary receptive cortex; diagonal lines, association cortex; white areas, phylogenetically new association cortex; small dots, motor cortex; stippled area, limbic system. (Reprinted with permission from Calanchini and Trout, 1971.)

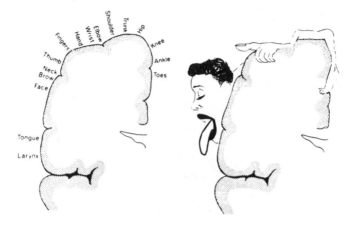

Figure 3. Section through sensorimotor area of one hemisphere with representation of sensorimotor activity in the component parts of the body. (Reprinted with permission from Calanchini and Trout, 1971.)

execution (praxis) of motor acts of the outer musculature. Representation of the body parts on the motor strip parallels that of the sensory strip fairly closely. Areas 6, 8, and 44 make up the secondary or premotor region. These premotor areas are well interconnected with the sensory association regions, thus making possible their principle function: the formulation of complex motor activities. The motor strip (area 4) has intimate cortical connections with the premotor (areas 6, 8, 44) and with the primary sensory strip (areas 1, 2, 3).

Split-brain Function

The two hemispheres of the brain are connected (communicate) via four commissures (joining fibers). The largest commissure is the corpus callosum (Figure 4). Severing the corpus collosom plus the anterior and hippocampal commissures permits each half of the brain to function independently without knowledge of what the other half may see, hear, feel, or do.

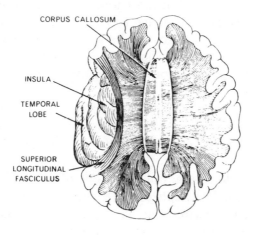

CORPUS CALLOSUM

INSULA

TEMPORAL LOBE

SUPERIOR LONGITUDINAL FASCICULUS

Figure 4. Horizontal section of the brain showing fibers of the corpus callosum and the superior longitudinal fasciculus, which runs from the lower frontal area into the temporal, parietal, and occipital regions. (Reprinted with permission from Calanchini and Trout, 1971.)

Such "split-brain" surgery is sometimes performed to alleviate severe epilepsy. When this is done, there is usually a significant decrease in seizures in both hemispheres simultaneously because of an inability of one hemisphere to excite the other. These patients seem to have no undesirable after-effects. Specialized testing of these patients led to the disclosure of split-brain functions.

In general, it has been found that the left hemisphere is dominant in almost all people. It controls language development and expression, skilled mathematical computations and analysis, and logical and analytical thinking. The minor, right hemisphere is able to understand simple language and to do very simple arithmetic. It is most highly developed for spatial relations and musical development. It may also be superior for functions such as imagination, music and art appreciation, dance and sculpture, geometrical and perspective drawing and visual perception.

Some left-handed people have their speech areas on the

right side of the brain, but most appear to have the usual left dominant hemisphere. Damage to the left temperoparietal areas in adults almost always results in aphasia (loss of speech and language). However, when damage occurs in young children, the language functions can be taken over by the right hemisphere.

Split-brain experiments were performed by Sperry (1970). A split-brain subject was seated in front of a screen to hide his hands from view. Several objects were on a table in front of him. The word "pen" was flashed for a tenth of a second in his left visual field so that only the right side of his brain could see it because the left fields of both eyes are connected to the right hemisphere; occipital areas 17, 18, 19. He could easily pick out the pen with his left hand from among the hidden objects by feel (also controlled by the right hemisphere; primarily areas 1, 2, 3, 4). However, he could not say what word had been flashed on the screen because language is a left-hemisphere function.

In another experiment, a word such as "toothbrush" was divided and flashed on the screen so that "tooth" appeared in the left visual field and "brush" appeared in the right visual field. When asked what the word was, the subject replied, "brush," because this word had projected to the left hemisphere, which also controls language. However, when asked what kind of a brush, he was unable to state, "toothbrush," but instead made all sorts of random guesses. The word "tooth," which had been projected to his right hemisphere, was unknown to the left half of his brain.

Other experiments have demonstrated that the left hand, controlled by the right hemisphere, can copy three-dimensional figures much better than the right hand of a split-brain patient. The right hemisphere has been found to be able to add simple numbers up to two digits but little beyond this, while the left hemisphere can perform more complicated mathematics.

The corpus callosum makes it possible for the two halves of the brain to communicate, permitting each half to develop unique functions. It also may permit brain asymmetry, which appears to have important consequences for learning, because asymmetry permits one hemisphere to be dominant.

Brain-wave studies also give evidence of asymmetrical cerebral function. The brain waves evoked in response to pure tones are larger in the right hemisphere, while those evoked in response to speech are greater in the left hemisphere. Thus, it appears that when the brain's language analyzer is used for speech or phonemic sounds, larger waves appear in the left cortex, while for meaningless sounds the brain waves are larger on the right. There is also some evidence that brain-wave asymmetry is correlated with intelligence. In general, bright and dull groups of children appear to be different with respect to hemispheric asymmetry. Essentially, no amplitude difference was found between the left and right brain waves in response to a stimulus in dull children. In bright children, on the other hand, significant differences were found (Callaway, 1975).

It is believed that some learning disabilities are related to lack of brain asymmetry and hemispheric dominance. Other learning problems are said to be produced by lack of proper communication between the two halves of the brain. As an example, Calanchini and Trout (1971) cite the case of the child who, "when blindfolded repeatedly elected to identify geometric shapes verbally and to place them in a formboard with his right hand," even if it meant changing the object from his left to his right hand. Both his right hand and his verbal identifications were controlled by his left hemisphere, therefore he did not have to shift hemispheres.

Evolutionary Hypothesis of Learning Disabilities

Calanchini and Trout (1971) have proposed a general hypothesis relating learning disabilties to brain function.

"The thesis proposed is that learning disabilities are cortical in origin and primarily a result of poor function in the phylogenetically (species development) and ontogenetically (individual development) newest and most complex areas of the brain. These areas, the prefrontal, inferior parietal, and inferior temporal regions, are the last to mature in the developing brain. According to this thesis, learning disabilities are a result of inefficient function in these or adjacent cortical areas. The inefficiency is more often an imperfection of nature than a result of actual insult to the brain. Just as the relatively fixed nearsightedness due to an imperfect eye can be compensated for by corrective lenses, so can the learning disability due to an inperfect brain be compensated for by properly selected teaching methods and learning habits.''

The concept is that the newest areas of the brain, both from an evolutionary and a maturational point of view, would be the most likely to vary in degree of development from person to person. Thus, the greatest differences should occur in those areas of the brain that were the last to develop both in an evolutionary (phylogenetic) and an embryonic (ontogenetic) manner.

The areas of the cerebral cortex that are of most recent origin phylogenetically include prefrontal areas 9, 10, 11, 45, 46, and 47 (Figure 2.) In the inferior (lower) parietal lobe, areas 39 and 40, and in the inferior temporal lobe, areas 20, 21, and 37, are phylogenetically new cortex.

THE SENSORY ANALYZERS

The cerebral cortex is considered to be the most highly organized part of the CNS. It is the part of the brain involved in conscious effort of all kinds. It also acts as a higher-level center for the analysis and integration of stimuli received from both internal and external sources. Feedback loops permit organisms to compare what they are doing with their intentions. This results in either modification of a program or its continuation or termination.

An examination of these feedback mechanisms may be made using Pavlov's concept of ''systems of analyzers and nuclear zones of analyzers in the cerebral cortex'' (Luria, 1966). These zones refer to those areas of the cortex where the greatest concentration of the neural elements of the analyzers and their connections are found. Outside of these nuclear zones there are other connections and elements that are functionally weak and diffuse in their actions.

The various cortical analyzers include the auditory analyzer, the visual analyzer, the motor analyzer, and the somesthetic analyzer. Signals reaching the sensory receptors in the skin, eyes, ears, etc., are subjected to preliminary analysis and selection at various subcortical levels on their way to the cortex. Some selection and perception occur at these subcortical levels. The signals then proceed to the primary receptive cortex for a given function (sensation, vision, hearing, etc.) where they are subjected to analysis by the first cortical analyzer. This analyzer subjects the incoming signals to complex analysis and integration.

Part of the proper functioning of this system involves the selection of the signals to be allowed to reach the cortical analyzers. Some selection is made by the inhibition of inappropriate information, such as background noises and sights. Such incoming (ascending) nonessential information may be blocked out by descending signals.

To the extent that a child's selection mechanisms fail to work properly, his consciousness will be bombarded with irrelevant signals that will confuse him. Often, hyperactive children appear to be suffering from just such an overload of irrelevant stimuli to which they react in random fashion. Thus, the random motor overflow seen in hyperkinetic children may be associated with this type of dysfunction.

The Auditory Analyzer

The primary receptive cortex of the auditory analyzer consists of area 41 and part of 42 (Figure 2). These areas contain the temporal gyri of Heschl where different sound frequencies (high or low tones) are received and analyzed (Figure 5). The high tones are received at the top of this region, medium tones at the central area, and the low tones at the bottom, as shown in the figure. This layout, according to frequencies, corresponds with a somewhat similar arrangement of frequencies found in the

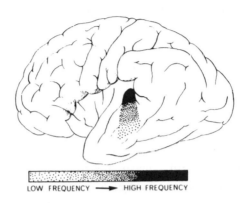

LOW FREQUENCY ⟶ HIGH FREQUENCY

Figure 5. Lateral surface of left cerebral hemisphere with the temporal lobe pulled down to expose Heschl's gyri and the distribution of tone frequencies. (Reprinted with permission from Calanchini and Trout, 1971.)

basilar membrane of the cochlea (organ of Corti) in the inner ear.

Speech and other complex sound signals appear to go from the primary receptive cortex to the association areas for further analysis. This association cortex is located in areas 21 and 22 and part of 42 in the temporal lobe (superior temporal gyrus) (Figure 2). Numerous neural connections extend from the association area by way of the fasciculus to Broca's speech region (area 44 of the left hemisphere) and to frontal areas 10 and 46 (Figures 2 and 4). These three premotor areas are concerned with the synthesis of articulation in the left hemisphere.

The cortical analyzer examines the patterns of frequency changes and sound sequences. These are the types of discrimination required to understand speech. Speech consists of sequences of vowels and consonants; the vowel sounds are tonal or harmonious and the consonant sounds are dissonant or atonal.

In speech, successions of phonemes tend to merge so that the brain has to be trained to distinguish them. These phonemes are the smallest units in the sounds of a language. Words are distinguished by the particular sequences of phonemes composing them. In the young developing child, the auditory analyzer (generally left hemisphere) programs the sounds (phonemes) of his language. When this has been accomplished, irrelevant sounds are ignored by being inhibited from reaching consciousness. This is why a person who first learned a foreign language has difficulty with those sounds in English that are not used in his language. These unfamiliar sounds tend to be blocked out or automatically inhibited, so that the person has difficulty hearing them. The same holds true for American-born children who speak a dialect. Therefore, some schools teach these native-born students English as a second language on the premise that a dialect may be considered similar to a foreign language in certain respects.

The effects of the inhibition of unfamilar sounds can be seen when students who speak a dialect attempt to distinquish pairs of English words. Seventy seventh-grade, lower socioeconomic, black students were given the Wepman Auditory Discrimination Test (Tarnopol et al., in press). Table 1 shows the word pairs that they had most difficulty distinquishing. In this dialect *e* and *i* are both pronounced like the *i* in "pin." Thus, both "pin" and "pen" are pronounced *pin*. Consequently, 70 percent of the group said that "pin" and "pen" sounded the same.

The incoming sound signals are too complicated for the human brain to analyze in complete detail. Consequently, exam-

Table 1. Wepman Auditory Discrimination Test. Percentages of 70 seventh-grade, lower socioeconomic, black students who said that these word-pairs sounded the same

Word pairs	Wrong replies (%)
sheaf-sheath	74
pen-pin	70
vow-thou	43
clothe-clove	36
bum-bomb	34
fie-thigh	31

ination of these sounds is done on the basis of past experience. It appears that the auditory analyzer attends to familar sounds and sequences based on the probability that they will have meaning. This probability is a reflection of prior learning. During a child's developmental years, different sets of similar sounds could lead to the same probability decision by the auditory analyzer. Thus, a child may mix up similar sounds, such as *d* and *t*, *f* and *th*, *v* and *th*, or *i* and *e*. These mistakes are common in younger children, but when they persist, they indicate the presence of a fundamental problem such as inhibition of the phoneme, or a neurological dysfunction. Examples of such errors are seen in Table 1. They include inability to distinquish sheaf-sheath, pen-pin, vow-thou, clothe-clove, and so forth.

Whitfield (1967) indicated that relatively little information is required to identify a speech sound: "Vowel sounds are characterized by the positions of two or three formant frequencies. The location of these frequencies is constant for a particular vowel irrespective of the speaker." The ability to understand words is based on both memory for the sound sequences in the words and the ability to retrieve these memories. Consequently, aphasia (inability to use or to understand speech) may be caused by errors in the auditory analyzer related to inadequate frequency analysis, sequential analysis, memory, retrieval, or any combination of these.

Secondary Association Cortex

Stimulation of the secondary auditory association cortex (areas 22 and 21 and part of 42) produces electrical brain potentials that spread to the frontal premotor cortex (areas 10, 44, and 46). On the other hand, stimulation of the primary auditory cortex (area 41 and part of 42) results in only localized electrical potentials.

The spread of electrical impulses from the secondary association cortex to the premotor cortex permits the auditory analyzer and the vocal cords to work together. In this way, speech and hearing are articulated.

The acquision of language in the young child involves combining what is heard with attempts to repeat the sounds. Thus, the understanding of language requires combining the working of the auditory analyzer with vocalizing the sounds. This process occurs during the child's first five years. Thereafter, a child can usually hear and understand speech without his own oral participation. However, when a child learns new complicated words, he will return to subvocal rehearsal of the words. If this process continues for ordinary language beyond kindergarten, it indicates either a maturational lag or dysfunction of the controlling brain areas. In either case, the child needs this crutch and should be permitted to use it.

When children begin to write, they once again use articulation to aid them in the perception of the exact sound sequence of each word. In doing this, the children are utilizing multisensory learning. They employ their auditory, kinesthetic, and visual memories simultaneously when learning to write. Copying letters involves visual perception and memory, and subvocalizing the letters involves both kinesthetic (muscle movements) and auditory (hearing) perception and memory. If this process continues beyond about age 8, it is probably necessary and should not be discouraged until assessment ensures that the child can function without this crutch.

This multisensory approach to learning language and writing is natural for children. It stems from the fact that the secondary divisions of the auditory cortex of the left hemisphere are directly connected with the premotor cortex used in speech (kinesthetic-articulatory analysis).

Dysfunction of Superior Temporal Area

During World War II, Luria (1966) had occasion to examine more than 800 patients with gunshot wounds in the language hemisphere of the brain who displayed some degree of disturbance to their speech discrimination. In general, such disturbances of phonemic hearing involved the left hemisphere for right-handed persons and the right hemisphere for left-handed persons. It was found that lesions of the upper portion (superior parts) of the (left) temporal lobe caused some form of aphasia. The most profound disorders of phonemic hearing tended to occur when the lesion was in the secondary association cortex. Such lesions tended to destroy the functioning of the auditory analyzer.

Table 2 shows the relationship between disturbances of phonemic discrimination and the area of the brain involved. In general, traumatic wounds in the zone of the auditory analyzer almost always disturbed phonemic hearing (95 percent of cases). As the areas affected were farther from the auditory analyzer, fewer cases of phonemic dysfunction were recorded. Finally, occopital, anterior (forward) frontal, superior frontal, and superior parietal wounds did not affect phonemic hearing. From this evidence, one may conclude that a child who exhibits defects of phonemic hearing has some form of dysfunction of the auditory analyzer or adjacent areas of the left hemisphere (if right-handed). Such dysfunctions may be caused by either damage or a genetic brain difference.

In general, patients with lesions of the temporal lobes have difficulty identifying sounds that are the same, because these

Table 2. Brain areas affected versus percentage of patients. Percentage of more than 800 patients with gunshot wounds of the brain who displayed disturbances of phonemic hearing (see Figure 2 for the brain areas)

Approximate brain areas	Percent
22, 41, 42, upper 21	95
Lower 40	53
37	37
47, 21	25
44	19
Upper 40	6
Upper 45	6
Upper 39	3
1, 2, 3, 4, 6, 8, 10, 17	0

(After Luria, 1966.)

sounds may appear different to them. Patients with lesions in the superior temporal part of the left hemisphere (areas 41, 42, and 22) usually have great difficulty repeating rhythmic taps if they are done quickly. When the taps are performed slowly, they can be counted out and reproduced.

In the most severe traumas to the auditory analyzer, the patients were unable to distinquish, repeat, or understand speech sounds. However, if the speech were supplemented by a visual presentation of the word, it could be repeated (if the visual cortex were intact). In milder cases, widely differing sounds could be understood and repeated but similar sounds caused trouble. When letter pairs such as *d-t, s-z, m-n,* or *p-b* were presented, there was a tendency to repeat the first letter twice, such as *m-m.* This problem of auditory discrimination is sometimes found in children with learning disabilities.

Luria (1966) summarizes, "It follows, therefore, that a lesion of the secondary divisions of the auditory cortex of the left hemisphere results in a disturbance in the ability to decipher the phonemic code, on which the process of analysis and integration of the sounds of speech is based."

Other speech-related problems may also occur when the auditory analyzer is dysfunctioning. These include difficulties with language concepts and pronunciation and also substituting words with similar sounds or meanings for a sought word (paraphasia).

As a general rule, the more complex forms of intellectual activity tend to be most affected by brain damage. However, in the case of lesions in the temporal lobe, patients with aphasia retain some degree of general intellectual functioning. They are able to retain certain abstract abilities such as classification functions and understanding metaphors, analogies, and causation within the limitations of their language deficits. Usually, nonverbal intellectual functions remain unimpaired. They may continue to be able to handle spatial relationships, geometrical constructions, musical composing and performance, and arithmetical operations that are not dependent on language.

Although such patients can understand logical or visual relationships, they are unable to perform a series of logical (arithmetical or language-based) operations if some data or results must be kept in mind. Moreover, *attempts to assist the process by speaking out loud impairs rather than improves their thinking.* In these cases, assistance may be sought in visual aids.

Writing   Traumas of the superior temporal region adversely affect writing. To be able to write, it is necessary to identify the phonemes of speech and to remember their correct order of presentation. Patients with lesions of the auditory analyzer can usually write words or phrases that are well established in their kinesthetic memory and can copy from printed or written materials. However, they are generally unable to write their own compositions or to write from dictation.

Reading   The ability to read may be seriously or completely impaired by lesions of the auditory analyzer. Defects in the discrimination and understanding of phonemes cause loss of understanding of the meanings of words. Major difficulties arise when attempting to decipher individual letters, phonemes, and words with which the person is not very familiar. Well known words may still be read, however.

Speech   Lesions of the auditory analyzer may also affect speech. In severe cases, the patient may lose the ability to understand the meanings of words. In milder cases, it may be difficult to uncover the problem. Sometimes word amnesia develops, so that the person cannot name an object that he does not see. Rehabilitation of such people is accomplished by presenting the object as its name is stated so that associations are formed (conditioning).

The ability to repeat a series of words or a sentence is often impaired. Loss of retention is often seen when words to be repeated by the patient are spaced 3 to 5 seconds apart. This seems to reduce drastically the person's ability to recall the word list. It has also been observed that nouns and adjectives are more readily lost in aphasia than are verbs, adverbs, prepositions, and conjunctions. Active parts of speech seem to be remembered better than things and their attributes.

In general, sensory aphasia results from dysfunction of the superior left temporal lobe. This is accompanied by disorders of the phonemic structure of speech, loss of word meaning, and memory for words. On the other hand, musical hearing and appreciation are generally unaffected. Conversely, lesions of the right temporal lobe may disturb the musical functions without affecting phonemic hearing.

Frequently, visual perception, spatial relations, kinesthetic perception, and memory are undisturbed. In these cases, rehabilitation may be based on the use of these intact sensory modalities.

Dysfunction of Middle Temporal Area

Lesions of the middle zone (areas 21 and 37) of the left temporal lobe cause auditory-memory failures (Luria, 1966). Penfield and Roberts (1959) stimulated these areas in patients during brain surgery. They found that their patients reported various memory images and hallucinations. They concluded that the middle temporal cortex mediated memory functions as well as some auditory analysis and interpretation.

Patients with lesions of areas 21 or 37 usually have no phonemic impairment, can repeat single words with good pronunciation, and can write such words from dictation, except when the words are complex or unfamiliar. Their main difficulties are related to auditory memory and sequencing. These patients exhibit marked difficulty with word or sentence spans given to them orally. They tend to be unable to reproduce more than one or two words. If asked to repeat several phrases, they may remember the first phrase but not the others. If a word series is presented and 5 or 10 seconds elapse with some unrelated speech, recall completely breaks down. These patients may be able to remember the words of a presented series, but they will be unable to retain the correct order.

These patients also tend to exhibit some difficulties with word meanings. Luria (1966) states, "For example patients who are asked to point to the eye and the ear may point many times to the ear and nose without noticing that they have made a mistake.'' These patients also tend to have difficulties when speaking involves ''seeking for words.''

Those who test children with learning difficulties will recognizc many of the same manifestations of auditory aphasia, perception, memory, and sequencing dysfunctions found in the brain-damaged population. From the nature of the auditory problem, one can estimate the area of the brain involved and perhaps the degree of involvement. In some cases the clinician will be dealing with traumatic brain lesions or a chemical disturbance, but in others there may simply be a genetic difference. These data together with intact functions will suggest the basis for remedial programs.

Testing for Auditory Dysfunction

Auditory dysfunction was one of the last sensory learning areas to be investigated as part of the learning disabilities syndrome. Until recently, very few adequate tests were available for the assessment of auditory perception and memory. Most test batteries relied on a test of auditory word discrimination, usually the Wepman Auditory Discrimination Test; a test of short-term memory, usually the Digit Span subscale of the Wechsler Intelligence Scales; and an omnibus test, the Illinois Test of Psycholinguistic Abilities. Other tests were available but were seldom used.

An important test of auditory perception that has not been sufficiently used is the Seashore Measures of Musical Talents (Seashore, Lewis, and Saetveit, 1960). Because it is primarily a music aptitude test, it is not always recognized as a measure of auditory perception. Wolf (1967) found that four of the six subtests of auditory discrimination measured by the Seashore test differentiated dyslexic from normal readers. These were the subtests of rhythm, time, tonal memory, and auditory blending, all of which differentiated at better than the 1-percent probability level.

Keir (Chapter 5) has developed a group of standardized, tape-recorded tests of auditory perception. He found that children with learning disabilities tended to have problems of auditory memory, auditory figure-ground, and auditory closure, in that order. A significant finding was that none of the 6- and 7-year-old children with severe auditory closure defects could do even the simplest blending.

Zigmond (1969) tested a group of 25 boys with reading problems and a control group of 25 normal readers. The boys all had at least average intelligence (IQ of 90 or more). They all had adequate hearing and visual acuity and were not emotionally disturbed. All had had normal educational opportunities and had no gross motor problems. They were given 15 tests to appraise auditory, visual, and intersensory abilities. All tests were chosen because they measured some function related to the acquision of reading.

There were six auditory measures, four visual measures, and five intersensory measures. The test results are shown in Table 3. The five auditory-memory measures and the auditory discrimination test significantly differentiated between the experimental and control groups, always in favor of the boys who were normal readers. The five intersensory measures also significantly discriminated in favor of the normal readers. Among the visual-perceptual measures, only Coding, which is a visual-motor test, discriminated.

The three pure visual measures did not discriminate. This concurs with the present authors' experience that only about 25 to 35 percent of the students with learning disabilities tend to have deficits of visual perception. On the other hand, more than 90 percent of these students tend to have visual-motor deficits.

The data also point to the significance of auditory memory as a factor in learning to read. Dysfunctions in the auditory analyzer appear to be a very significant cause of reading problems.

Lindamood Auditory Conceptualization (LAC) Test An interesting and useful new test is the Lindamood Auditory Conceptualization (LAC) Test, (Lindamood and Lindamood, 1971). This test may be used at all ages from kindergarten on and is individually administered. The test has two categories,

Table 3. Means, *t*-values, and probability levels for auditory, visual, and inter-sensory measures. Twenty-five dyslexic boys compared to 25 boys with normal reading ability

Test	Dyslexics (mean)	Controls (mean)	*t*-score	*p*
Auditory				
Digit span	5.0	6.2	4.67	0.001
Word Span	4.1	4.8	3.88	0.001
Memory for Sentences	64.1	76.2	3.74	0.001
Memory for Rhythms	11.3	14.0	3.11	0.01
Discrimination of Rhythm Pairs	21.3	24.6	3.02	0.01
Nonsense Word Span	4.4	4.8	2.28	0.05
Visual				
Coding	47.4	56.4	2.91	0.01
Block Design	52.5	60.7	1.14	NS
Visual Discrimination	5.5	6.1	1.09	NS
Memory for Designs	8.6	8.8	0.64	NS
Auditory Stimulus-Visual Response				
Oral Directions	9.1	12.4	2.92	0.01
Matching Dot Pattern and Rhythm	10.4	12.2	2.77	0.01
Visual Stimulus-Auditory Response				
Syllabication	9.9	16.9	6.25	0.001
Visual Digit Span	4.8	5.8	3.74	0.001
Picture Span	3.6	4.1	2.21	0.05

NS, not significant; *p*, probability level from *t*-score.

with a gradual increase in the complexity of the sound patterns in each. In the first part of the test, the subject must discriminate each sound heard and determine whether they are the same or different. The subject places a block for each sound heard in a row, using the same color when the sounds are the same and different colors to indicate different sounds. A sound pattern might be *b b s,* which would call for two blocks of the same color followed by one of a different color. Any colors may be used.

In the second part of the test, the subject uses blocks in the same way to represent the sound patterns within syllables. For example, *zat* would call for three blocks of different colors. The real test comes when the sound patterns are changed by omissions, substitutions, or additions. Thus, *zat* could be followed by *zaf,* in which case the subject would have to observe the change and replace the last block with one of a different color.

Lindamood and Lindamood have found that children with no "auditory conceptualization" defects can pass the entire test but that both children and adults with such deficiencies fail this test. Their research has disclosed high correlations between LAC test scores and Wide Range Achievement Test Reading and Spelling combined scores at each grade level from kindergarten through grade 12 ($r = 0.66$ to 0.81). They have also developed a remedial program to go with their test.

Goldman-Fristoe-Woodcock (G-F-W) Test   A new battery of auditory tests has been released by Goldman, Fristoe, and Woodcock (1975). The battery includes the G-F-W Auditory Selective Attention Test, Diagnostic Auditory Discrimination Tests, Auditory Memory Tests, and Sound Symbol Tests. The tests are supplied on tape with easel kits containing the visual components of the tests. Normative data are available from age 3 to beyond 80 years.

VISUAL PERCEPTION

Visual perception refers to our interpretation or understanding of what we see. Clearly, a neonate can have little understanding of what he sees, so that perception must be the result of experience. However, there also appear to be some inherent aspects to visual perception. For example, newborn animals that can walk and infants who can just crawl appear to exhibit depth discrimination. In the well known "visual cliff" experiment, neither the animals nor the infants could be coaxed out onto a plate of heavy glass that could support them, because the glass was 3 feet above the ground. It was found that infants who wore a patch over one eye also refused to crawl out onto the glass, indicating that monocular cues were sufficient for the infants to discriminate depth.

Visual perception is probably determined by learning, together with the different forms, shapes, angles, and movements to which neurons respond. Some insight into the development of perception may be gained from studies of people who were blind with cataracts from birth and first gained sight as adults after surgery. Such patients seem to be able to distinquish colors (but not by name) and figure-ground relationships. They cannot identify familiar objects by sight until they feel the objects, and they are not even able to state which of two sticks is longer without resorting to feeling them.

To test the effects of experience on visual perception, Canadians (of European ancestry) from environments based on vertical and horizontal lines (streets and buildings) were tested against Cree Indians from an environment that included all orientations: their summer tents had diagonals and their winter lodges had vertical and horizontal lines. Both groups were tested for visual acuity of patterns in different orientations. The Canadians were able to resolve the vertical and horizontal orientations better than the diagonals. The Cree Indians proved to be equally good at this task in all orientations. This difference in visual acuity for the two groups was considered to be the result of learning in different environments.

Children with cerebral palsy and other motor handicaps may also have difficulty conceptualizing diagonals and forming the diagonal lines in letters such as *A, K, M, N, X, Y,* and *Z.* To help these children learn to make these letters, physical therapists hold the children so that their bodies slant to get the feel of the diagonal concepts. Because perception of the external environment tends to be based on comparisons with one's self or body image, such exercises are considered helpful.

Children with learning disabilities sometimes have disorders of visual perception. They may have reversals, such as failure to distinquish *b, d, p, q,* or reading *saw* for *was.* If not corrected, these reversals may persist into adulthood. They may have closure problems, so that they are unable to complete a partially seen word such as *p-rtial.* Some children have spatial-relation deficits, so that maps are meaningless and they have difficulty finding their way around in school buildings. They sometimes appear to have form constancy problems, so that the same object seen at different times or from different angles confuses them. They may also have figure-ground problems that cause difficulty distinquishing foreground from background. This may manifest itself as an inability to find a geometrical design that is hidden inside a larger design.

Klees (1976) stated, "Children presenting figure-ground impairment, which is always associated with an overall picture of perceptual difficulties, remained severely maladapted to the ordinary school environment, despite individual psychological and pedagogic help, if their IQ's were below 110. Children with the same problem but higher intelligence, managed (provided their emotional balance was satisfactory) to gain enough benefit from the curative measures to compensate for their school difficulties." The figure-ground test used was a subtest of the Developmental Test of Visual Perception (Frostig et al., 1963). Klees continued, "On the other hand, children presenting perceptual difficulties without figure-ground impairment recuperated more easily, even with an IQ as low as 90."

The Visual Analyzer

In humans, the left half of the retina of each eye is connected to the left side of the visual cortex at the rear of the brain (area 17) (Figure 2). Similarly, the right half of each retina goes to the right half of area 17. The left visual field is seen by the right retinas (the image being reversed by the lens). The image is then projected to the right half of the visual cortex (Figure 6). This type of image projection on the brain makes possible the special depth effect of binocular vision.

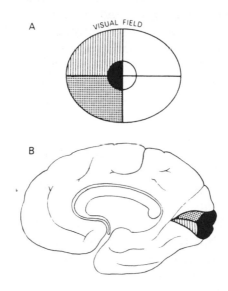

Figure 6. A, human visual field; B, medial surface of the right cerebral hemisphere showing the representation of the left visual field on the striate cortex. (Reprinted with permission from Calanchini and Trout, 1971.)

The more important a sensory function is, the greater the area of the brain devoted to that function. Thus, the focal spot in the eye (fovea or macula) takes up only about 1 percent of the retina, but it projects to almost 50 percent of the visual cortex. This makes it possible to analyze an object in great detail by focusing on it.

In the primary visual analyzer (area 17 on the striate cortex of the occipital lobe), neurons respond to the simpler forms such as lines and edges. Cells in the secondary visual analyzer (areas 18 and 19) respond to more complex forms, including angles, rectangles, movement, and so forth. All of these different forms tend to be coded by individual neurons in the visual cortex. Some cells respond to a single shape at rest, while others respond only to the shape in motion.

Hubel and Wiesel (1965) studied vision by placing a microelectrode capable of contacting single neurons in a cat's brain. They identified the two types of cortical neurons described above as simple cells and complex cells. The simple cells were found to fire a spike discharge whenever the appropriate shape (vertical line of a given length, for example) was in a circumscribed field of view. A complex cell might also respond to this same shape, but it responded regardless of where the shape was in the cat's visual field. This continued firing of the complex neuron appears to result from connections between the complex cell and a number of simple cells. Each simple cell fires when the shape is in its given part of the visual field, thereby stimulating the complex cell to continuous firing as long as the shape is visible.

Projections from Visual Analyzer   The main neural projections from the primary visual analyzer (area 17) are to the adjacent secondary analyzer (areas 18 and 19). From the occipital region (areas 18 and 19) there are important connections with the lower (basal) temporal cortex (areas 37 and 20) and to the prefrontal motor cortex (area 8). The superior occipital area 19 projects to the adjacent superior parietal area 7 (sensory association) and to areas 39 and 40 (inferior parietal). These projections indicate the ways in which visual-auditory, visual-motor, and visual-sensory associations are made (Calanchini and Trout, 1971).

From animal experiments one finds that stimulation of the primary visual cortex (area 17) seems to limit the excitation to that particular field. However, stimulation of area 18 produces widespread excitation to the projection areas, and it appears that local stimulation of area 19 creates an inhibitory effect over an equally extensive area.

Stimulation of the occipital region of humans during operations indicates similar results. Penfield and Roberts (1959) observed that stimulation of area 17 created elementary visual sensations such as fog, flames, colored rings, etc., while stimulation of areas 18 and 19 led to more complicated sensations, including visions of past experiences.

Visual Analysis: Occipital Region   Lesions of the primary area of the visual cortex (area 17) lead to constriction of the visual field but do not greatly impair complex visual perception. Such lesions result in various degrees of central blindness, depending on the amount of area 17 destroyed. However, with areas 18 and 19 intact, the secondary analyzer continues to function and compensates for the impairment created by constriction of the visual field (Teuber, 1960).

If the lesion involves the secondary analyzer (areas 18 and 19) but not other areas, visual acuity appears to be intact, but the perception and recognition of objects are reduced (visual agnosia). In severe cases of optic agnosia, the person cannot recognize either objects or their pictures by sight but may still be able to identify them by feel. Luria (1966) has observed that in moderate cases of visual agnosia, patients can recognize simple or familiar objects but have difficulty with more complicated ones. Visual identification of something involves the recognition and integration of a number of cues. Patients with agnosia tend to pick out some cue and then try to guess what the object is. They generally attempt to determine what it is by "a method based on verbal logic." This often gives the wrong result because they do not have enough important signs under study. As examples, a picture of a pair of eye glasses was called a bicycle; a rooster with bright feathers was interpreted to be a fire (red feathers were said to be flames). In cases in which the disturbance of visual perception is minor, the defect may appear only if a series of lines are made through the line-drawing of an object (Figure 7). A similar problem of identification may occur if pictures are presented in quick succession.

Observation of the drawings of patients with visual agnosia demonstrates that the primary disability is one of synthesis of the perceived parts into a whole object (Luria, 1966). The tendency is for the person to see isolated visual signs of parts of an object or picture, but they are unable to put the parts together in the correct places to form an integrated whole. For example, when drawing a man the patient may draw a number of parts reasonably well (line drawings), but one arm may be attached to

Figure 7. Some children have difficulty drawing around the outlines of the circle and the square, especially in the presence of confusing lines. This would constitute a visual figure-ground deficit for those failing, if 95 percent of the children tested at the same age could outline the designs.

the head and the other may be off in space; similarly, the nose, ears, and mouth may be detached from the figure. Often, stick figures are sketched with no body (legs to head). Some of these inappropriate aspects of drawings may be found in the sketches made by children with learning disabilities. It is not uncommon in these drawings to find some parts of the body missing and others displaced (Figure 8). Because patients with bilateral wounds of the occipital lobes may present rather severe cases of this form of optic agnosia, it may be concluded that the less extensive problems often demonstrated by children with learning disabilities are probably related to occipital lobe dysfunction of lesser degree.

Lesions of the occipital region of the subordinate hemisphere (usually right) often result in an inability to remember faces (agnosia for faces). The person is able to copy drawings but is unable to reproduce them from memory. Children with learning disabilities often have disturbances of this type.

Occipitotemporal Lesions   If a patient can copy drawings adequately, it may be assumed that there is no dysfunction of the visual analyzer (occipital lobe). If there is no problem involving phonemic analysis, the auditory analyzer appears to be functioning well (temporal lobe). However, if there is a lesion in

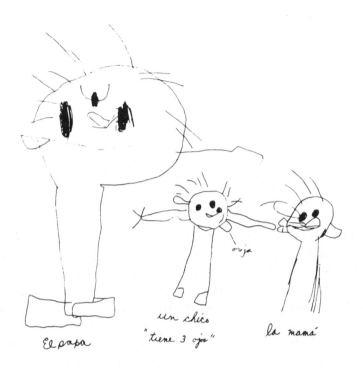

El papa

un chico
"tiene 3 ojos"

la mamá

Figure 8. Peter, age 6 years, 3 months, drew his father, his mother, and a child. The child has three eyes, *tiene 3 ojos*. Arms and legs are attached to the head. This is normal for younger children. At this age it indicates possible self-image and visual-perceptual immaturity or dysfunction. (Reprinted with permission from Gorriti and Rodriquez Mūniz, 1976.)

the inferior temporo-occipital area of the left hemisphere (areas 19 and 37), it may affect the ability to describe pictures or objects verbally. At the same time, the visual images tend to be somewhat unstable. Patients with a lesion in this region may not have an auditory discrimination problem and may be able to blend words adequately. They may also be able to write quite well. However, they may exhibit great difficulty remembering the meanings of words. This disability is thought to be related to a disturbance in the connections between the visual images of words and their names or meanings. This was demonstrated by asking patients to copy drawings, which they could do well enough. However, when they were asked to make drawings without copying, they were unable to do so (Luria, 1966). It appears that the words are unable to call up the appropriate visual images. Patients with lesions confined to the superior temporal region do not have this problem.

Children with learning disabilities sometimes exhibit similar problems. They may be unable to convert an auditory pattern (heard word or tapped-out rhythm) into a visual image and reproduce it in writing. Writing the word, drawing the picture, and reproducing the rhythm in written form introduces another group of sensory modalities (visual-motor, auditory-motor). These must also be tested to determine if they are intact.

Spinelli and Pribram (1966) have also shown the important influence of the inferior temporal cortex on the visual system. Feedback from this cortex assists visual discrimination and problem-solving ability in monkeys.

Sometimes people who can distinquish colors visually are unable to identify them verbally. This may occur when visual-auditory associations are impaired. The person will be able to match colored discs but will be unable to name the colors. When this defect occurs in an adult as a result of brain damage, it is usually accompanied by a reading problem. This type of inability to name colors has been described by Geschwind (1966) as the result of a severance of the speech cortex from the visual cortex.

Occipitoparietal Lesions   Patients with bilateral lesions of the occipitoparietal regions (areas 19, 39, and 7) had no severe visual agnosia. They could also tell the difference between an object and a picture of the same object. However, they were unable to see more than one object at a time. When presented with two or more objects, regardless of size, they could only distinguish one of them; the other objects disappeared into the background (Luria, 1966). This problem was accompanied by visual ataxia (inability to move eyes smoothly among the objects viewed). If a picture contained several figures and one was pointed out to the patient, he would be unable to fixate the figure. The ataxia caused his gaze to shift about in an uncontrolled manner. Thus, he would lose sight of the figure. This, of course, severely limits both visual perception and imagery. Such patients have great difficulty reading or following a story depicted by a series of pictures.

It was found that a patient with a bilateral occipitoparietal wound could not write well with his eyes open because of the effects of visual-motor ataxia. However, when his eyes were closed, his writing improved measurably (Luria, 1966). It was also found that a small dose of a stimulant (caffeine) improved the functioning of this patient for about 30 to 40 minutes. He was then able to see two figures at the same time instead of only one. Whereas previously he had been unable to place dots near the center of a circle (pencil and paper test), with caffeine he could perform this task fairly well. Thus, two methods of assisting these patients were demonstrated.

Occipitofrontal Functions   Spinelli and Pribram (1966) have demonstrated the influences of the frontal association cortex on occipital functions in monkeys. Areas 8, 18, and 19 work together to coordinate the visual optic reflexes. These reflexes control the voluntary and involuntary movements of the eyes in eye-tracking functions. These functions include both reading and studying objects or scenes in a coordinated manner. Sometimes children with learning disabilities are found to have problems on tests of eye tracking. Their eyes may not track smoothly (ataxic jumping), or they may scan in both directions instead of from left to right. These children need assistance in learning to use their eye muscles in a controlled, meaningful way.

TACTILE AND KINESTHETIC ANALYZERS

Tactile sensations and analyses are performed in the cortex behind the central fissure (areas 1 and 3) (Figure 2). The amount of cortex devoted to sensory connections to each part of the body is proportional to need. Therefore, an enormous area of the sensory cortex is devoted to the lips, tongue, hand, thumb, and fingers, while much less area is given to the back and shoulders (Figure 3). Each cortical region connects to the opposite side of the body, so that stimulation on the left is sensed by the right brain, and vice versa.

Sensations that are deeper in the muscles and body involve the proprioceptors. These give us the senses of position and movement. They tell us what the peripheral (striate) muscles are doing; what movements the arms, legs, and body parts are making. This analysis is called kinesthesis and is mediated by area 2. Because the tactile and kinesthetic senses are so closely related cortically, they tend to work together; however, it is possible for one to be defective but not the other.

The tactile and kinesthetic (somesthetic) analyzers make it possible to discriminate weights, to identify pressure differences such as hard and soft, to distinguish objects by feeling (stereognosis), to know what parts of the body are touched, and to tell which different body areas are touched simultaneously, as in two-point discrimination tests. Children with learning problems sometimes have tactile or kinesthetic deficits that reduce their potential for learning through these modalities.

Dysfunction of the tactile analyzer arises from lesions, inherited differences, or chemical imbalances in the parietal lobes. Such deficits are referred to as tactile agnosia, or astereognosis. It has been noted that lesions in the areas constituting the secondary tactile analyzers leave elementary forms of tactile feeling and pain intact. However, the ability to synthesize sensations and to distinguish objects and shapes may be lost. Such patients could respond to discrete touch sensations well enough, but they could not perform two-point discrimination or distinguish circles, crosses, or numbers drawn on their skin (Luria, 1966). Such defects have been shown to result from focal lesions in brain areas corresponding to the body areas affected (Figure 3).

THE SENSORIMOTOR ANALYZER

The primary sensorimotor analyzer is in cortical areas 1, 2, 3, and 4 (Figure 2). The premotor regions of the frontal hemisphere include association areas 9, 10, 44, 45, and 46. The secondary association zones of the motor analyzer include areas 1, 2, 5, and 7 in the parietal lobe and premotor areas 6 and 8 in the frontal lobe.

The sensorimotor analyzer and its association areas are the most complex of the mechanisms for analysis and synthesis. "Disturbances in the working of the motor analyzer may therefore develop from lesions in the most widely separated parts of the brain" (Luria, 1966). The development of both gross motor and fine motor acts utilizes information supplied by all of the analyzers. Children develop voluntary control of movements by utilizing feedback from their visual, auditory, kinesthetic, and tactile systems, including the use of speech and language to help mediate this process. The kinesthetic analyzer furnishes important information concerning the positions and movements of the muscles and joints involved in the action. Automatic, learned motor acts are monitored by kinesthesis and tend to be taken over by the cerebellum in many cases.

The motor analyzer (area 4) appears to integrate the mass of feedback information involved in the control of smooth muscular movements. In performing this function, it must synthesize spatial (right-brain), language (left-brain), and tactile-kinesthetic communications. Calanchini and Trout (1971) state, "The realization that a motor act is not just an efferent (output neurons) phenomenon but is highly dependent upon afferent (input neurons) information from all the major sensory modalities leads to the recognition that the entire brain is involved in movement. *This helps explain why most children with neurological learning disabilities have motor involvement, regardless of what part of the brain is involved.*"

In general, about 90 percent of the children with learning disabilities appear to have motor coordination and/or visual-motor deficits. In Silver's study of 150 children with reading disabilities, 92 percent had deficits on the Bender Visual Motor Gestalt Test (cited in Tarnopol, 1969). In a study by Clements et al. (1971), 84 children with minimal brain dysfunction (MBD) (learning disabilities) were compared with a control group of 45 normal children. Slow, poor, labored handwriting was found in 98 percent of the MBD children and in none of the controls.

Evidence of kinesthetic-motor deficits predictive of learning disabilities may be found in children from birth. Inability to suck the nipple adequately during the first days after birth is a very early sign of a child at risk who should be followed with careful observation. Sucking appears to be the first instinctive response to stimulation in the facial area developed by a human fetus. It should be well developed at birth.

Difficulty with small muscle movements appropriate to the child's age is diagnostic. Observations may include things such as tying shoelaces, buckling a belt, sewing, using scissors, threading a needle, and so forth. Problems involving the use of large muscles may also appear, such as clumsy or inadequate walking, running, skipping, or throwing.

Impairment of the kinesthetic-motor analyzer may also affect speech. This may be seen in the form of articulation problems and stuttering. According to Calanchini and Trout (1971), "Since speech plays a vital role in the development of neural circuits for reading and writing, impaired kinesthetic analysis and synthesis may well be an underlying cause in the learning problems in some children. A kinesthetic-motor component may also be present in the auditory-articulatory analysis required to write. As a result, reading or spelling aloud may be more difficult than silent reading or written spelling, because of the added necessity to use auditory-articulatory and kinesthetic feedback mechanisms."

Luria (Chapter 2) discusses in detail the participation of speech in the formation of children's motor acts. From about age 2, signals derived from speech are part of the means by which children control their motor activities in the learning stages. At first, the helping signals come from an adult's instructions, and later they appear in the form of self-commands utilizing speech.

In summary, the motor analyzer works in conjunction with a large number of association and premotor auxiliary analyzers. Afferent signals come to the primary analyzer (area 4) from three major sources. Some impulses come from the auditory-speech zones to help regulate voluntary movements. Other signals come from the muscles, joints, and the vestibular apparatus (equilibrium centers) to be integrated with the regulating speech signals. A third group of communications arrive from the visual-spatial analyzer to be integrated with the other two sets of signals. Together these afferent impulses are analyzed by the motor analyzer and synthesized into a coordinated voluntary act. The voluntary action results from efferent neural impulses from the motor analyzer. Dysfunction in any part of this complex of signals will prevent smooth functioning of this "kinetic melody" and cause discoordination in the muscular movements.

Lesions of the Postcentral Cortex of the Motor Analyzer

Lesions in areas 1, 2, 3, 5, and adjacent areas of 7 in the parietal lobe are in the postcentral zone of the sensorimotor analyzer. Such lesions produce sensory loss in the corresponding projection areas of the body and a reduction or loss of afferent signals to the motor analyzer. The result is an afferent or kinesthetic apraxia, ranging from paralysis when severe to mild discoordination when minimal.

Localized lesions in areas 1, 2, and 3, the primary sensory cortex, cause both sensation loss in the corresponding muscles and surface areas and also motor defects. The motor incoordination appears to be the result of the loss of afferent information from the muscles to the motor strip. This seems to cause the efferent commands from the motor strip to go astray. As a result, when attempting to contract the biceps of the arm, for example, both the biceps and the triceps may contract simultaneously and result in an abortive movement.

Other problems that may arise from dysfunction in these areas include inability to place the fingers in various positions upon request or to move the fingers in any given manner. Voluntary control tends to be lost.

When the lesion is in area 5, similar problems occur. Smooth movements are disrupted. However, the movements can sometimes be made with the aid of visual control.

Dysfunction in left hemisphere (dominant) areas 1, 2, 3, and 5 generally produce an apraxia as described above in the right (contralateral) upper limb. This makes fine movements, such as threading a needle or writing smoothly, impossible. At the same time, difficulties sometimes also arise in the left (ipsilateral) limb. Difficulties in imitating an examiner's movements or in showing how to open a door become apparent in mild cases when vision is excluded or the door must be imagined. Such patients can open a real door but cannot demonstrate how to open an imaginary door.

A localized lesion may produce a specific apraxia rather than a generalized disturbance. For example, an oral apraxia may occur in which speech movements are impaired. Tests of lip and tongue movements reveal this condition. Such patients may have great difficulty performing indicated movements or in repeating a series of movements. They can be helped to overcome these deficits by observing their lips and tongue in a mirror as they practice the exercises.

All of these apraxias have been found in some children with learning problems, usually in mild form. The use of a mirror to assist children with speech articulation problems is well known.

Lesions of the Postcentral Cortex and Motor Aphasia

Lesions in the left hemisphere of the lower parts of areas 1, 2, 3 and damage to area 40 tend to produce defects of articulation. The main effect on the patient's speech is a confusion of certain articulations involving consonants such as *k* and *t*. Other errors come from substituting similarly articulated consonants such as *b* for *p*. These patients may also have great difficulty repeating tongue twisters such as "She sells sea shells on the seashore."

Luria (1966) states, "The fact that in afferent motor aphasia speaking (or reading) aloud may be more severely affected than reading by the patient to himself is explained by the nature of the principal defect—disturbance of the ability to analyze and integrate the kinesthetic signals that comprise the basis of speech."

Functions such as writing, and in some cases reading and comprehension, may be disturbed. These functions are related by the fact that when first learning to write, children use articulation to help analyze the sounds of words. Pupils in the first and second grades in Russia were tested in writing and spelling. It was found that the number of errors made was increased five to six times when the children were not permitted to articulate the words (Luria, 1966).

Patients with severe forms of these types of motor aphasia may be unable to write or to identify different sounds. They may make the errors of substitution of like articulated consonants previously noted when writing. It has been found that these patients can be greatly assisted by pronouncing words out loud while they observe their tongue placement in a mirror. These methods have also been used effectively in helping some children with learning disabilities.

Premotor Lesions

Premotor area 6 is of especial interest. In lower animals the motor and premotor regions form a common entity. They first separate in evolution at the level of the carnivores. In lower monkeys, area 4 occupies about four times the cortex of area 6. However, in adult humans the reverse is true; area 6 consumes three times the cortical space of area 4. Finally, by age 4 the neuronal development of area 4 is complete, whereas that of area 6 takes until age 7 to mature. This age coincides with the observed maturation of the visual-motor processes measured by such tests as the Frostig Developmental Tests of Visual Perception (Frostig et al., 1963). Further evidence of the importance of area 6 is indicated by the fact that stimulation of this cortex has a very widespread effect ranging to areas 1, 4, 5, 8, and 39, while stimulation of area 4 spreads only to adjacent regions.

The premotor areas of the cortex appear to mediate the organization of movement. Once an action has begun, impulses from this area are able to stop it or to change it to another mode of action. They also organize individual motor movements into smooth, skilled acts. Lesions in the premotor region tend to reduce or to destroy these various possibilities. Such lesions do not affect the ability to perform simple, individual movements. Instead, the movements become clumsy or discoordinated, thus impairing complex motor acts. When the lesions invade subcortical regions, compulsive movements in the form of motor perseveration appear.

Patients with premotor lesions have no problems reproducing stationary positions of the fingers and hand, for example. However, coordinated complex movements disintegrate. Typists may lose fluency of action and resort to typing with one finger; handwriting tends to disintegrate; and musicians may lose their facility of movement required for a smooth performance. When asked to raise and lower his hand at a given signal, the patient may raise his hand but not lower it. He will have to be told to lower his hand. When asked to use both hands simultaneously, the patient may fail either by using his hands in succession or by not using one hand. The hand omitted will generally be the one opposite the lesion (contralateral hand). While tapping out rhythms is relatively easy for patients with postcentral lesions, those with premotor lesions have considerable difficulty with this task. Sometimes minor speech difficulties appear that impair fluency, causing the speech to become fragmented.

Efferent Motor Aphasia

Lesions of the lower (inferior) parts of the left premotor cortex produce efferent motor aphasia. The regions included are Broca's area 44 and adjacent zones. Such lesions are accompanied by profound disturbances of speech.

These patients are frequently able to articulate individual sounds, and they can write the letters of the alphabet from dictation. Problems arise when they try to say words and phrases requiring the control of a series of articulations. They have difficulty both in constructing a smooth series of sounds and in inhibiting preceding articulations to make the change from one sound to the next. For example, if the word *friend* is started *fr*, the person may continue to repeat *fr fr*, as in stuttering, and have difficulty transferring to the next syllable. Writing also causes problems. Even though these patients may be able to write individual letters, they are unable to write words; they cannot get the order of the letters correct in words, tending to perseverate on beginning letters or syllables.

Another manifestation of motor aphasia is telegraphic speech. A series of nouns tends to be substituted for phrases and sentences. Luria (1966) cites the case of a soldier, with a gunshot wound in area 44, telling how he was wounded: "Here ... front ... and then ... attack ... then explosion ... and then ... nothing ... then ... operation ... splinter ... speech, speech ... speech." After recovery, these patients retain elements of telegraphic speech, and their speech tends to remain flat and inexpressive.

When the lesion is in front of Broca's area 44 (areas 45, 46, and 47) grammatical structure and phrasing are retained and telescopic speech does not occur. Difficulties may arise when attempting to repeat a series of words or phrases or during conversation with another person. The sequence of the word series to be repeated may be deranged, and some evidence of perseveration may occur. In conversation, echolalia tends to occur, so that the patient repeats the question put to him as part of the answer. Answers are abbreviated. These patients have great difficulty repeating a series of words or numbers in reverse. They also have great difficulty retelling a story they have read or in making up a story from a picture.

Luria (1966) indicates that it is possible to correct these deficiencies. This is accomplished by the use of props. Questions may be used to develop a story, and a series of drawings on cards may be used to help the patient gain fluency of expression.

Lesions of the premotor region also cause certain intellectual deficits. Although the meanings of words and simple sentences are retained, difficulty is encountered when attempting to understand complex sentences and concepts. These patients tend to have difficulty with coding tests in which symbols are placed beneath numbers. They fail to learn which symbols go with which numbers to speed the process. They may tend to add and subtract by units instead of automatically. Thus, it would take longer to add 2 + 5 than 5 + 2. These problems appear to be related to the disintegration of internal speech.

Some children with learning disabilities have difficulty when requested to repeat a series of digits or words in reverse or to retell what they have read. Many children with learning problems experience difficulty with the Coding subtest of the Wechsler Intelligence Scale for Children (WISC). Some continue to perform addition and subtraction on their fingers. In all such cases, a detailed analysis of each child's method of learning and his possible sensory learning deficits is recommended. Based on the results of this analysis, an appropriate teaching method should be prepared for each child. It is to be expected that this type of help will materially reduce the problems of learning-disabled children.

LITERATURE CITED

Calanchini, P. R., and Trout, S. S. 1971. The neurology of learning disabilities. In: L. Tarnopol (ed.), Learning Disorders in Children: Diagnosis, Medication, Education. Little, Brown, Boston.

Callaway, E. 1975 Brain Electrical Potentials and Individual Psychological Differences. Grune & Stratton, New York.

Clements, S. D., Davis, J. S., Edgington, R., Goolsby, C. M., and Peters, J. E. 1971. Two cases of learning disabilities. In: L. Tarnopol (ed.), Learning Disorders in Children: Diagnosis, Medication, Education. Little, Brown, Boston.

Frostig, M., Maslow, P., Lefever, D. W., and Whittlesey, J. R. B. 1963. The Marianne Frostig Developmental Test of Visual Perception. Consulting Psychologists Press, Palo Alto, Calif.

Geschwind, N. 1966. Color-naming defects in association with alexia. Arch. Neur. 15:137.

Goldman, R., Fristoe, M. and Woodcock, R. W. 1975. Goldman-Fristoe-Woodcock Auditory Skills Test Battery. American Guidance Service, Minnesota.

Gorriti, C. J., and Rodriquez Muñiz, A. M. 1976. Learning problems in Argentina. In: L. Tarnopol and M. Tarnopol (eds.), Reading Disabilities: An International Perspective, pp.27–37. University Park Press, Baltimore.

Hubel, D. H., and Wiesel, T. N. 1965. Receptive fields and functional architecture in two non-striate visual areas (18 and 19) of the cat. J. Neurophys. 28:229–289.

Klees, M. 1976. Learning disabilities in Belgium. In: L. Tarnopol and M. Tarnopol (eds.), Reading Disabilities: An International Perspective, pp. 85–96. University Park Press, Baltimore.

Lashley, K. S. 1929. Brain Mechanisms and Intelligence. University of Chicago Press, Chicago.

Lindamood, C. H., and Lindamood, P. C. 1971. Lindamood Auditory Conceptualization Test. Teaching Resources, Boston.

Luria, A. R. 1966. Higher Cortical Functions in Man. Basic Books, New York.

Luria, A. R. 1972. The Man with a Shattered World. Basic Books, New York.

Penfield, W., and Roberts, L. 1959. Speech and Brain Mechanisms. Princeton University Press, Princeton.

Seashore, C. E., Lewis D., and Saetveit, J. G. 1960. Seashore Measures of Musical Talents. Psychological Corp., New York.

Sperry, R. W. 1970. Perception in the absence of neocortical commissures. In: Perception and Its Disorders. Res. Pub. ARNMD, Vol. 48. Association for Research in Nervous and Mental Disease.

Spinelli, D. N., and Pribram, K. H. 1966. Changes in visual recovery functions produced by temporal lobe stimulation in monkeys. Electroenceph. Clin. Neurophys. 20:44.

Tarnopol, L. 1969. Introduction to children with learning disabilities. In: L. Tarnopol (ed.), Learning Disabilities: Introduction to Educational and Medical Management, Charles C Thomas, Springfield, Ill.

Tarnopol, L., Breed, J. S., Tarnopol, M., and Ozaki, M. Learning disabilities and minority adolescents. Bull. Orton. Soc. 27. In press.

Tarnopol, L., and Tarnopol, M. (eds.). 1976. Reading Disabilities: An International Perspective. University Park Press, Baltimore.

Teuber, H. L. 1960. Visual Field Defects after Penetrating Missile Wounds of the Brain. Harvard University Press, Cambridge.

Whitfield, I. C. 1967. The Auditory Pathways. Williams & Wilkins, Baltimore.

Wolf, C. W. 1967. An experimental investigation of specific language disability (dyslexia). Bull. Orton Soc. 17:32.

Zigmond, N. K. 1969. Auditory processes in children. In: L. Tarnopol (ed.), Learning Disabilities: Introduction to Educational and Medical Management. Charles C Thomas, Springfield, Ill.

Chapter 2

Cerebral Organization of Conscious Acts:

A Frontal Lobe Function

Aleksandr R. Luria

Several years ago, two of the most outstanding psychologists of our day, B. F. Skinner and D. O. Hebb, proposed decoding the well known abbreviation CNS as "conceptual nervous system."

At first this was a mere joke. Now, however, the idea seems reasonable. The human brain not only recodes sensory information, turning it into a system of concepts, but also establishes human plans and programs and formulates the conscious control of human actions. The brain is really an organ of freedom (conscious behavior), and it would be unwise to ignore this basic feature by approaching the human brain with the same concepts and methods that one approaches the brain of the rat.

The question arises, is it possible to find ways of understanding the basic qualities of the human brain without following the old mentalistic approaches or repeating the mechanistic ideas that were popular a generation ago? How can one obtain a

From a lecture presented to the XIX International Congress of Psychology, London, 1969.

scientific solution to the riddle posed by man's free activity and conscious behavior? To find a solution to this problem, one has to start analyzing the concrete relations of the child with his immediate social enviroment. This was the approach taken by the late famous Soviet psychologist L. S. Vygotski and this is the way the present discussion shall follow.

A newborn child starts life with a series of innate, self-regulating systems of a very elementary type: breathing and sucking, primitive orienting reflexes, and a battery of early forms of motor activity. These elementary forms of activity were studied by a number of eminent scholars from Schelovanov, Minkowski, Peiper, and others to the recent brilliant investigations by Jerome Bruner. But how far these forms of behavior are from the conscious and self-controlled conduct of a school child or an adult!

The newborn child starts life in social contact with adults. The mother speaks to the child. She shows the child an object, pointing to it and saying, "This is a doll," and the child looks at the doll. She says, "Give me the doll," and the child tries to do it. Originally, the child's conscious action is divided between two persons; it starts with the mother's command and ends with the child's movement. But during the subsequent period of the child's development, the structure of this action begins to change. The child starts using his own language by saying, "Dolly!" He singles out the object named, turns his eyes to the doll, and tries to grasp it. The child's own speech begins to serve as a command, and the function, formerly divided between two persons, now becomes a new form of inner, self-regulated psychological process. This is the start of a new type of behavior, social in origin, verbally mediated, and self-controlled.

ORIGIN OF CONSCIOUS BEHAVIOR

Luria shows the development of normal children from about 6 months to 5 years of age in terms of their abilities to follow directions and to control their own actions by means of self-commands. Often children with learning disabilities are retarded in their development, so that they may be slower than normal in accomplishing these various abilities. The tests used by Luria may indicate possible approaches to testing children for retarded development, suggesting high risk for possible learning disabilities (the editors).

The development of the highest forms of conscious, self-regulated behavior is neither a simple process nor a leap from a "field-reaction" to free behavior. The first acquisition of a command-controlled action is the start of a long process in the development of the higher psychological functions. Below are some simple experiments which try to establish a basic model for the development of a child's self-controlled behavior.

It is well known that an adult's command may evoke an orienting reaction in a child 6 to 8 months old and a simple motor action in a child 10 to 12 months old. If one names an object placed in the child's immediate enviroment, the child will turn his eyes toward the object. If one says, "Lift your hands," the child will do it. An oral command can start the child's action, but the command is not as yet able to overcome the influence of the immediate enviroment. It cannot stop an action already started by the child, nor can it construct a new program that could control his behavior.

Consider a situation in which a small plush rabbit is placed before a child and he is allowed to play with it; then a new toy is added, for example, a rubber hen. Now the command, "Give me the rabbit," fails to get a proper response. The child turns his eyes toward the rabbit, but they meet the attractive hen, and the child grasps this new toy. The child's behavior, originally controlled by the oral command, is now blocked by an orienting reaction to a novel stimulus.

The same can be seen if one tries to use an oral instruction to arrest an action already started by a child or to change it for another one.

Now consider placing two objects, a rabbit and a hen, close to a child 14 to 16 months of age and repeating several times,

"Give me the rabbit." Then, without changing the intonation, command, "Give me the hen." The inertia of the evoked action at this stage is so intense that one is often unable to change it and overcome the previous stereotype; hearing the new order, the child continues to repeat his previous action.

The following experiment shows how an oral instruction gradually assumes its controlling function. Two familiar objects are placed in front of the child, a wooden cup on his right and a wooden box on his left. The child sees that a penny is placed under the cup; then the instruction follows, "Give me the penny." A child of 1 year, 6 to 10 months will fulfill this instruction. Some difficulties are observed if the fulfillment of the command is delayed for 20 to 30 seconds. In this case the oral instructions may easily lose their directing role and the child may begin to examine both objects, grasping the object named in only 50 percent of the cases. The immediate orienting reaction suppresses the memory of the oral order; only at the next stage of development do the memory traces of the earlier perception and oral order become stable so that a selective action may take place.

REALIZATION OF ORALLY DIRECTED PROGRAMS

At the early stages of development, the oral command can start an action but is unable to overcome the immediate influences or the inertia of established stereotypes. This rule may be illustrated by experiments with a simple motor reaction. If a child of 1 year, 8 months to 2 years, 2 months is given a rubber balloon connected to a pneumatic recorder and is told, "Press the ball," the result will not be as simple as might be expected. If the plastic bulb itself does not evoke a grasping reflex, the child will start to press the balloon but will be unable to stop the reaction; a series of successive pressures will be recorded over a considerable time period. All efforts to stop these uncontrolled movements will be futile. If the child is ordered to press only when he is told to do so, the child is unable to stop his movements. While hearing the command, "Don't press any more," he may often increase the pressure. The oral command may start the action, but it is as yet unable to arrest it.

The weakness of the controlling function of an oral instruction at this stage manifests itself even more distinctly in experiments with an orally conditioned motor reaction.

The instruction, "When you see a light, you must press the bulb," seems to be extremely simple, but as a matter of fact it includes a complex program of actions. A preliminary plan must be established; the immediate orienting reaction to the stimuli must be blocked; the stimulus light must acquire a conditional meaning; and the programmed movement must be started after the signal appears. The realization of this complex program proves to be impossible for a child of 2 years to 2 years, 6 months. After the words, "When you see a light," the child immediately begins to look for it and stops any bulb-pressing movements, but when he preceives the end of the instructions, "... you must press the bulb," he starts the motor reaction (bulb pressing) regardless of the signal. The selective influence of the oral instruction is not yet ripe, and no realization of a complex orally formulated program is possible.

The same can be seen even in children of 2 years, 8 months to 3 years if the instructions are made complex and if a complicated program with a conditional choice reaction is established.

The child is given the following command, "When you hear a sound, press twice," or, "When you see a red light, press the bulb," or, "When you see a green light, don't do anything." In such cases a child of 3 or even 3.5 years will easily retain the verbal instruction but will still be unable to follow this program. In the first experiment, he will respond to the sound with a series of uncontrolled pressures; in the second, he will press when he sees both the positive and the negative signals. Only at the age of 3.5 to 4 years does the child become able to perform this complicated program, blocking the immediate influence of the stimulus. However, even a slight complication in the experiment results in a breakdown of this form of self-controlled, conscious behavior.

DEVELOPMENT OF ORAL CONTROL OF ACTIONS

Now the basic question is asked: Is it possible to speed up this process and to find means of improving the conscious control of the child's own actions at early stages of his development? All attempts to improve the child's control of his behavior at the age of 1 year, 6 months to 1 year, 10 months have failed. However, experiments with children of 2 years, 6 months to 2 years, 8 months produced some interesting results and indicated some ways of solving these problems.

At this stage of development one is still unable to insure the child's immediate control of his own behavior; however, one can observe some positive results when the child's motor reactions evoke a feedback signal that provides him with information concerning the result of his action. If the child were instructed to press the bulb in order "to put out the light," superfluous pressures would disappear. The same could be observed in older children when, after the command, "If you see the light, you will press twice," every pressure resulted in a feedback acoustic signal. Thus, at this early stage of development, an oral program could be carried out only if it were reinforced by a feedback signal of the action taken.

Now the question arises, couldn't this feedback signal be replaced by the child's own controlling activity and the child's own speech, his own oral commands, used as the means of control?

The first experiments with children of 2 years, 4 to 8 months gave negative results. A child of this age could easily respond to each stimulus with the simple verbal reaction, "Go!" But if one instructed the child to accompany his own command by a motor reaction (pressing the bulb), the child's oral command did not yet have a controlling function. After giving himself the order, "Go!" the child either stopped the motor reaction or continued the superfluous pressures despite his own command.

Quite different results were obtained in children of 3 years, 2 to 6 months. The introduction of the child's own command, "Go!" had no success in the first stages of the experiments, but after some training the child's motor reactions became coordinated with his oral commands. When saying, "Go! Go!" the child began to produce organized motor responses (pressures) and to block the superfluous uncontrolled movements. Cancellation of these oral commands resulted in a reappearance of the superfluous motor reactions.

The same was observed when a group of somewhat older children was asked to press twice in response to every signal and the child's own command, "Go! Go!" was included. In all of these cases, the child's oral system, which was now based on more concentrated excitatory processes than the motor system, assumed controlling functions. The first manifestations of overt speech were observed as the "highest regulator of human behavior."

However, it would be erroneous to suppose that at this stage of development the child's conceptual nervous system is developed well enough to control his conscious actions. To prove it is not, one need only make the experiments a bit more complicated and pass from simple motor reactions to a complex program with a choice of reactions. Here the psychological pattern of behavioral control changes; a positive signal (green light) must evoke a motor reaction, while a negative signal (red light) must block it. The psychophysiological role of the child's oral commands undergoes a fundamental change here as well. The positive command, "Go!" must start a motor reaction, while the command, "No!" acquires a negative semantic meaning but preserves its immediate excitatory influence. The question arises, which influence will predominate, the immediate excitatory influence or the semantic blocking? Experiments with children of 3 to 3 and-a-half years answer this question. In many children of this age, their own command, "No!" not only blocks the motor reaction, but even disinhibits it; saying, "No!" the child may increase the pressures.

The same can be seen in a more grotesque form in imbecile children of a much older age; in this case the verbal self-command, "No!" results in a stronger discharge of the motor reaction. This means that there is a stage when the motor-discharging role of the child's own oral command dominates the semantic role of his speech and that further development is needed to make the semantic aspect of the child's speech predominant. This stage is reached at the age of 4 to 4.5 years, when the child begins to form some inner programs of complex actions and when his own overt speech becomes a less decisive factor. Here, the semantic programs based on the child's inner speech begin to acquire their controlling functions, and the child becomes able to fulfill the programs of simple choice reactions without his own overt verbal reinforcement. This stage may be regarded as the first step toward the consolidation of the inner controlling mechanisms of the child's conscious actions and perhaps as the first stage of the controlling functions of the "conceptual nervous system."

> Children with learning disabilities may exhibit delays in the ages at which they are able to perform the functions described in the above research by Luria and Polyakova. These delays may be maturational, in which case performance of the tasks will appear at a somewhat later age. In some cases, however, the delays may be caused by neurological dysfunction, either damage or genetic differences. In these instances, learning may require the development of alternate neural pathways or sensory systems in order to reach the same level of development as a younger child. In some instances, the use of verbal self-command may even disrupt the child's ability to develop the controls described. Such cases of overloading were described in Chapter 1. On the other hand, it has been found that the use of oral self-commands may be used successfully to help many older children learn to do many things that are otherwise too difficult for them (the editors).

BASIC PRINCIPLES UNDERLYING THE
FUNCTIONAL ORGANIZATION OF THE HUMAN BRAIN

The second problem is: Which structure of the human brain plays a decisive role in establishing plans and in realizing programs of behavior? Which basic systems of the brain ensure the selective attention and the permanent control of the highest forms of man's purposive actions? The present author proposes a first approach to this problem. As a result of nearly 40 years of work in the field of neuropsychological analysis of focal brain lesions, this author has obtained a series of basic data that can be used in this discussion. This discussion will try only to bring them together rather than to speculate on an ultimate theory.

To say that the human brain operates as a whole makes both a correct and an erroneous statement. It is correct because the most complex forms of human actions require the participation of all brain systems; it is erroneous because it can hardly be suggested that the human brain works as an undifferentiated whole. Modern data concerning brain morphology, physiology, and neurology require that the idea of the brain as a homogeneous unity be discarded. There is every reason to approach the human brain (including its cortex) as a complex functional system that includes the joint work of different levels and areas, each of which plays its own role. The concept of a "working constellation" advanced by Ukhtomsky, as well as the concepts of a "functional system," "dynamic localization of functions," or Hebb's "cell assembly," have since assumed much more definite meanings than at the time they were originated.

Data obtained during the last decades provide grounds to single out at least three basic blocks of the human brain, each making its own contribution to their common work.

Energy and Tone Block

The first block may be called the *block of energy and tone*. It includes the upper brain stem, the reticular formation, and, to a certain degree, the oldest parts of the limbic cortex and hippocampus (Figure 1). This block is responsible for the stable tone of the cortex and for the state of vigilance that some psychiatrists erroneously call "consciousness." The basic forms of activity of this block have been discussed in the publications of Jasper (1959), Lindsley (1960), Magoun (1958), and Moruzzi (1954). Their analyses of the changes in sleep and wakefulness, in arousal and drive, may be regarded as the most significant contributions to our science. This block includes a considerable amount of curious neurons that react to every change of stimuli and that Jasper calls "attention units."

The present author had the opportunity to analyze the behavioral changes occurring in patients with lesions of the medial parts of the brain cortex and brain stem, and he observed in these patients marked disturbances in stable wakefulness, instability of memory traces, and selective organization of thinking similar to those observed in dreamy states (Luria et al., 1967; Luria, Podgornaya, and Konovalov, 1969*). However, these lesions never resulted in any basic disturbances of the structure of concepts, nor did they result in a primary loss of the simple programs that control conscious action. In these cases a slight reinforcement, increasing the lowered cortical tone, might easily lead to a compensation of the defects and to a recovery of the deranged control of behavior (Homskaya, 1970).

Although the participation of the first block in the common work of the brain is of great significance for the higher forms of conscious activity, there are no grounds to consider it to be a mechanism that is specific for the realization of programmed actions.

Hyperkinetic children with learning disabilities often appear to have dysfunction in the energy and tone block. The symptoms of hyperkinesis include random, uncontrolled, and almost con-

---

*References in languages other than English are omitted from the "Literature Cited" section and are marked with an asterisk in the text. Please write to the editors for a complete list of foreign-language references (the editors).

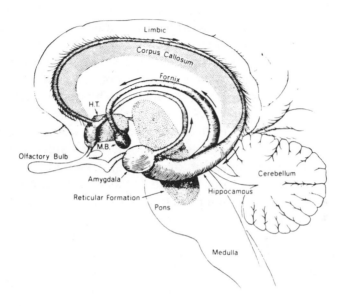

Figure 1. Representation of the limbic system, upper brain stem, and cerebellum. M.B. is mammillary body, H.T. is hypothalamus. (Reprinted with permission from Calanchini and Trout, 1971).

stant overactivity, short attention span, impulsivity, fluctuating behavior, and low frustration tolerance. These symptoms may become either partly or completely ameliorated by appropriate stimulant medication. It is hypothesized that in some cases these conditions are related to a low central (reticular) arousal level. In such cases, the cerebral cortex is thought to be receiving insufficient tonic stimulation from the arousal mechanism in the reticular formation, leading to behavior that the child cannot control. A stimulant drug, which selectively increases the function of the reticular activating system, improves the cortical tonus, thus permitting the child to regulate his behavior consciously. Thus, a dysfunctioning energy and tone block may produce hyperactivity that may often be helped by appropriate stimulant medication (the editors).

Information Block: Input, Coding, and Storage

The second block of the brain includes the posterior parts of the hemispheres with the occipital, parietal, and temporal regions as well as their underlying structures. It can be defined as a *block for the input, recoding, and storage of information* received from the external and proprioceptive worlds. It is well known that the systems of this block are highly modality-specific. The occipital lobe, being a central device for visual analysis, does not take part in the decoding of acoustic signals, while the temporal lobe participates only in a limited and specific form in the organization of visual information.

Each system entering this block has a hierarchical structure, and the work of each primary (extrinsic) zone is organized by a superimposed secondary (intrinsic) zone with highly developed upper levels of "associative" neurons. A series of very important studies showed that only a small part of the neurons of these zones are of the nonspecific type of "attention units," while the greater part perform a highly specific function firing to isolated cues of different modalities. The specificity of these areas decreases with the transition to the "tertiary zones" of the cortex or to the "areas of overlapping," which include units reacting to different modalities and which provide a synthesis of serial influences to some simultaneous schemes. The roles of these areas in the elaboration of complex forms of spatial and conceptual structures are analyzed in Chapter 1 and in Luria (1961, 1963, 1966).

One basic feature is to be emphasized. Patients with lesions of the posterior parts of the brain may lose several important behavioral operations, but these lesions never result in a general deterioration of their conscious conduct. These patients retain their plans and their strategies; they are fully aware of their defects; and they very actively try to overcome them. They remain human beings in the full meaning of the word, and, in spite of their tragic fate, they never lose their conscious forms of conduct. It may be concluded that the second basic block of the brain, no matter how important it may be, is in no way responsible for the regulation and control of man's conscious behavior.

Planning and Control of Behavior Block

The third block of the brain includes the frontal lobes and is of particular interest for the basic problem of this discussion. *The frontal lobes of the brain are the last acquisition of the evolutionary process and occupy nearly one-third of the human hemispheres.* They preserve a vertically organized structure typical of the motor zones (Polyakov, 1965*), and their anterior parts possess some distinctive features of the most complicated tertiary zones. They are intimately related to the reticular formation of the brain stem, being densely supplied with ascending and descending fibers. Their mediobasal parts may be regarded as an important cortical structure superimposed on the systems of the upper brain stem (French, Herhandes, and Livingston, 1955; Nauta, 1952*, 1964). They have intimate connections with the motor cortex and with the structures of the second block, but in contradistinction to the latter, their work is not of a modality-specific type. As shown by a group of Russian scholars, *their structures become mature during the fourth and fifth years of life, and their development makes a rapid leap during the period which is of decisive significance for the acquisition of the first forms of the conscious control of behavior* (Glezer, 1959*; Kononova, 1940*).

There are many reasons to suppose that this block of the brain plays an important role in the realization of the plans and programs of human actions and in the regulation and the control of human behavior. The present author has considered this question in a series of publications (Luria, 1969*; Luria and Homskaya, 1966*), and the findings are summarized below.

FRONTAL LOBES AND REGULATION OF CONSCIOUS ACTIONS

Neurologists are aware of the general kinds of behavioral disturbances that are caused by severe lesions of the frontal lobes. On the other hand, limited lesions may be poor in symptoms because of certain equipotentiality of the foci of the prefrontal area (this "highest and least differentiated part of the human cortex," as formulated by Hughlings Jackson).

Patients with severe lesions of the prefrontal areas, as a rule, do not manifest any stable alterations of memory and orientation in the immediate environment such as those that are typical of patients with lesions of the medial parts of the hemispheres. They do not suffer defects in perception, movement, speech, or even logical operations. At first glance, one may suppose that they preserve all the basic functions of the human brain; but this is not the case. Closer observations show deep disturbances in the regulation and control of the conscious behavior of these patients.

As a rule, only a limited number of these patients are able to plan or to follow programs, nor can they preserve complicated motives for their conduct. No strategy can be observed in their behavior, and they do not try to find proper ways or means of fulfilling a given task. Complex forms of behavior are, as a rule, replaced by primitive "field actions," impulsive responses to immediate stimuli, or an inert reproduction of previously evoked stereotypes that, at first, were meaningful but have become totally senseless in the new conditions.

The classic description of the behavioral changes in animals after the destruction of their frontal lobes (beginning with the early publications of Bianchi and Jacobsen and ending with the latest findings of Anokhin and Pribram) has been enormously enriched by observations carried out on patients with massive lesions of the frontal lobes.

The present author cannot forget one of his patients, a woman with a massive bilateral tumor of the frontal lobes, who at an early stage of her disease was seen to stir burning coal with a broom and to cook some of the bristles instead of noodles. And another patient, a soldier with a massive bilateral gunshot wound of the frontal lobes, who started to plane a plank but could not stop and automatically continued his work until almost a half of the bench itself was planed away.

It is easy to see that no defective movements were responsible for such strange alterations of behavior. Massive derangements of inner plans and programs predominated in these cases, and the purposeful forms of conscious behavior were replaced by uncontrolled responses to immediate impressions or by automatic inert stereotypes.

Although children with learning disabilities rarely exhibit the bizarre types of behavior described by Luria in the cases of patients with serious frontal lobe lesions, some of these children do show behaviors reminiscent of those described. Perseverative acts are often observed in children with learning disabilities. Such children, when asked to draw a line between two points on a sheet of paper, may continue the line to the end or even off the paper. Some of these children tend to perseverate in their speech and repeat the same thing over and over. In some instances, a child's behavior has been characterized as bizarre by a clinical psychologist who may have attributed it to some psychodynamic cause. Here is evidence that neurological dysfunction may produce these anomalies (the editors).

FRONTAL LOBES AND REGULATION OF VIGILANCE

To realize a complicated program, one has to preserve a certain level of vigilance. It is well known that complex discursive activity can hardly be performed in a dreamy state; but a general excitation of the cortex caused by impulses coming from the reticular formation is by no means sufficient in this case. The activity required for the realization of a complex program must be highly selective; it must be evoked by a definite goal or plan; the information that is related to the given plan has to be singled out and must become dominant, while all outside impressions must be suppressed. Such selective organization of the active state can be ensured only by close participation of the highest cortical areas and their descending fibers.

The frontal lobes, especially their medial parts, are exceptionally rich in descending and ascending fibers of the reticular formation; this was shown in a series of works by French, Herhandes, and Livingston (1955), Nauta (1958, 1964), and others. One might therefore expect that the subject's strong intention can mobilize the apparatus of the brain stem and, with the help of the activating system, raise the activity level of the frontal parts of the brain: and one might expect that lesions of the frontal lobes may result in a breakdown of these activating influences. Both assumptions have proved to be right.

The first assumption was corroborated by a series of brilliant experiments by Walter (1953, 1966*) and Livanov, Gavrilova, and Aslanov (1966). It is well known from Walter's studies that any expectation of a signal evokes special kinds of slow potentials that appear in the subject's frontal lobes and subsequently spread to the posterior parts of the cortex. Walter called them "expectancy waves" and observed their intensification, when the subject's activity increased, and their disappearance, when the instruction was canceled.

At the same time, Livanov, using a 50-channel amplifier, made an important observation. When the subject started solving a difficult intellectual task (such as multiplication of two-digit numbers), a significant number of synchronously excited points appeared in his frontal lobes; they disappeared when the problem was solved or canceled. The same could be observed in excited paranoid patients; the synchronously excited foci in the frontal cortex disappeared after the patients were treated with a tranquilizing drug (chlorpromazine). These data make it very probable that the frontal lobes of the human brain play an important part in the regulation of vigilance required for the realization of complicated intellectual tasks.

Livanov's observation that chlorpromazine suppresses the development of synchronously excited brain waves in the frontal lobes of paranoid patients and that these excitations appear when normal people solve difficult intellectual problems indicates a possible reason for a well known phenomenon. When hyperkinetic children are given tranquilizers, their intellectual efficiency tends to be impaired. The same is true of adults under psychiatric treatment. In one case, a college student who earned all A grades in mathematics began to fail the biweekly tests. It was found that her psychiatrist had prescribed a tranquilizer for anxiety. When the psychiatrist refused to stop the medication even temporarily, she had to drop the course. Chlorpromazine is known to block the dopamine receptors in the brain. This tends to reduce the transmission of the neurotransmitter dopamine in certain nerve synapses. The reduction of transmission by these nerves may help account for the decreased intellectual efficiency. Stimulants, on the other hand, tend to have the opposite effect, stimulating transmission and improving memory (the editors).

The facts mentioned were obtained on non-brain-damaged subjects. It is highly probable that in patients with severe lesions of the frontal lobes, regulation of the higher forms of vigilance may be markedly disturbed. This problem has been studied by Homskaya in this author's laboratory in a long series of experiments on patients with frontal lesions. Some of her findings are reviewed below.

It is well known that any stimulus will evoke a series of somatic reactions in a normal person that are symptoms of arousal or components of an orienting reflex, such as constriction of the blood vessels of the fingers, dilation of the vessels of the head, and a galvanic skin reaction. These somatic changes persist for some time and are extinguished when the subject becomes habituated to the stimulus. They can be increased and prolonged if a special instruction is given; for example, if the subject is asked to count the stimuli, to await some change in them, or to press a key when a stimulus appears; in other words, when the stimulus assumes a "signaling meaning."

Such an increase and fixation of the vegetative components of the orienting reflex are observed in normal subjects and in patients with lesions of the posterior part of the hemispheres; but they are not observed in patients with lesions of the frontal lobes and especially of their medial or basal parts.

These patients may exhibit immediate vessel reactions to changes in stimuli, but the oral instructions mentioned do not evoke any stabilization of the vascular symptoms of the orienting reflex. This is of great diagnostic significance and often is the only symptom of a frontal lobe lesion.

Similar data were obtained from experiments in which electroencephalogram (EEG) components of the orienting reflex were recorded. It is well known that any new and unexpected stimulus requiring increased attention results in a decrease of the alpha band of the EEG (8 to 12 cycles per second (cps)) and especially of its high frequencies. It is likewise known that an oral instruction imparting a special meaning to the signal makes this suppression of alpha waves more pronounced and more stable.

The same is observed in patients with lesions of the posterior parts of the hemisphere. No such effect is seen in patients with lesions of the frontal lobes, especially of their mesial parts. The oral instruction to count the stimuli or to await their changes does not increase the effect of desynchronization, and in some cases a slight suppression of the lower frequencies or even a paradoxical exaggeration of the alpha band takes place.

During the last few years, a new EEG symptom of activation has been carefully studied and proven to be highly reliable. As shown by Genkin* and later by Artemieva and Homskaya*, a careful analysis of the structure of the alpha waves in a normal subject discloses a peculiar change in the asymmetry of the length of the ascending and descending fronts of the alpha waves. These fluctuations are periodic and follow each other in cycles of 6 or 7 seconds. This regularity is observed in the quiet state of a normal subject and is violated when activation or intellectual arousal takes place. The same can be observed in patients with lesions of the posterior parts of the brain, but no such breakdown of the regularity of this asymmetry index is observed in patients with lesions of the frontal lobes.

Perhaps of greatest importance are data obtained from experiments with evoked brain-wave potentials conducted by Simernitskaya and Homskaya* on normal and brain-lesioned subjects. It is known that each specific stimulus (visual or tactile) evokes specific potential (voltage) changes in the occipital or sensorimotor parts of the cortex and that the expectation of such a stimulus results in an exaggeration of these evoked potentials.

The same effect, produced by the oral instruction to await a signal, is seen in patients with lesions of the posterior parts of the hemisphere; but no such effect of an oral command is seen in patients with lesions of the frontal or mediofrontal parts of the brain. These data show that the frontal lobes play a significant part in the regulation of the active states started by an oral instruction.

> It is well known that children with learning disabilities often have attentional deficits. These and other problems and their relationship to brain waves are described in Chapter 3 (the editors).

FRONTAL LOBES AND REALIZATION OF PROGRAMMED ACTIONS

Disturbances in the regulation of vigilance observed in patients with severe lesions of the frontal lobes exert far-reaching influences on the structure of man's conscious actions. Being unable to sustain permanent selective attention, patients of this group become unable to fulfill complicated programs of action. Only patients with massive bilateral lesions of the frontal lobes and with a pronounced akinetic syndrome are unable to fulfill the simple instruction, "Lift your hand!" The difficulty of effecting this command increases when the patient's hands are under the bedsheet, so that he has to execute a complex program of successive movements; first to free his hand and then to fulfill the instruction. In these cases, he often answers, "Yes, I shall lift my hand," but does not perform any movement at all.

As a rule, patients with severe lesions of the frontal lobes can easily imitate simple movements performed by the psychologist, such as lifting a fist or a finger. But the picture completely changes if the task is made more complex, as when the oral command comes in conflict with the visually presented pattern. For example, a patient may be given the following order, "When you see my fist, show me your finger." In this case, the realization of the program will be impossible; and, although the patient retains the oral instruction and repeats it, after one or two correct reactions the directing role of the oral command breaks down and the required movement is replaced by an imitative reaction. The same can be observed if the patient is asked to respond to every single knock with two knocks and to every two knocks with a single one. The patient's inability to maintain a program organized by a verbal code and the reduction of his action to the level of imitation occur in both cases.

The breakdown of an action controlled by an oral program may assume a different form when the conscious action is replaced by an inert stereotype. For example, a patient may be instructed to lift his right hand in response to one knock and his left hand in response to two knocks. A patient with a less severe lesion of the frontal lobes is often able to carry out this instruction. But if this stereotype is broken as in R—L—R—L—R—L—L, the patient will preserve the stereotyped order and will continue the alternation already started, regardless of the signals given, even though he retains the verbal instruction. In cases of massive lesions of the frontal lobes, this pathological inertia manifests itself even at the verbal level. If the patient is instructed to fulfill a simple program, for example, to produce one strong knock and two light ones and to accompany these actions by his own oral commands (strong—light—light), he often begins to change his commands. He adds perseverative repetitions of one of the links;

and saying, "Strong—light—light. Strong—light—light—light," he acts out this deformed program in his motor reactions.

It is obvious that in these cases the patient's own speech is unable to regulate his behavior. Data show that *the breakdown of the oral control of behavior in patients with severe lesions of the frontal lobes brings about the same phenomena that was seen when discussing the early stages of development of the highest forms of conscious actions.*

The breakdown of conscious actions and their replacement by inert stereotypes or primitive reactions to immediate impressions can be analyzed in experiments with graphic responses to given programs. For example, drawing a figure involves the execution of a series of successive movements; to draw a cross, the subject has to draw a vertical line and then switch his movement to a horizontal one. In order to perform a more complex program, such as to draw a circle and a cross, he has to perform a series of movements. After drawing the circle, he must move his hand to another place on the sheet, and only then can he start drawing the cross. It can be seen that the fulfillment of this program requires that the previous movements, as well as all outside influences, must be blocked.

If the lesion is located in the deeper regions of the frontal lobe, the patient may start drawing, but the completion of the program may be prevented by motor perseveration. In the case of severe damage in the prefrontal zone, the patient may be unable to carry out the intermediate link of the program not mentioned in the instruction. In the execution of the command, "Draw a circle and a cross," he may fail to shift his hand and both figures will be superimposed. Sometimes the execution of the program is violated in a different link; the patient may not shift from one unit of the program to another, sticking to the first action and replacing the program with an inert stereotype.

Finally, the realization of the program may be violated by uncontrolled outside influences or extraneous associations. A patient with a traumatic cyst of the frontal lobe was instructed to draw a square. He began to do it, but instead he drew three quadilaterals and then a big square following the borders of the sheet of paper.

The psychologist conducting the experiments whispered to his colleague, "Have you read that a pact was signed today?" The patient immediately reacted to this by writing in the middle of the quadrilateral "....Act. N." "What is the patient's name?" the psychologist asked his assistant, and the patient immediately wrote, "Yermolov." "Look, this is so similar to the behavior of lobectomized animals" whispered the psychologist, and the patient added to the already written word "Act" the words "on animal breeding..." One could hardly find an example that could better express the breakdown of the patient's programmed action.

Here is another example of the same kind. A patient with a massive tumor of the left frontal lobes was asked to draw a triangle. He drew it at once, but added a second one. Then he was asked to draw a minus sign; he drew an oblong, perseverating on the closed form of the triangle. When he was asked to draw a circle, he did it, but he additionally drew the same oblong in the middle of the circle and wrote the words, "Entrance strictly forbidden!" (Figure 2). Can you guess what the patient's former occupation was?

The analysis of the basic types of breakdown of programs in patients with severe lesions of the frontal lobes opens up new vistas in the neuropsychology of conscious action, its inner structure, and its cerebral organization.

> Although the problems of patients with severe frontal lobe lesions may not be found among children with learning disabilities, many of the difficulties which these children manifest appear to be related to the types of problems described by Luria. For example, perseveration when drawing geometrical designs is often found. On psychometric tests, these children may evidence an inability to plan ahead and to carry out a plan. For example, to do well on the subscales of the Wechsler Intelligence Scale for Children (WISC), an adequate plan must

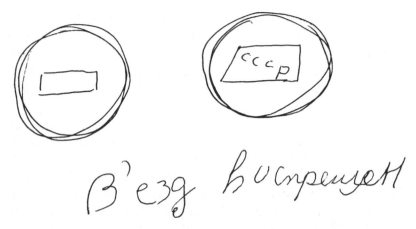

Figure 2. Drawings by a patient with massive tumor of left frontal lobes. The patient was asked to draw a circle. He drew two circles with oblongs inside and USSR in one oblong. Then he wrote below the circles, "Entrance forbidden." A circle with an oblong in the center is the international symbol for "Entrance forbidden" (one-way street). Thus, one may surmise that the patient's occupation was chauffeur.

be formulated and followed, as on the Object Assembly Sub-scale, where visual-perception appears to be the sensory modality most involved. However, the formation and carrying out of a plan of attack is also most important in the solution of these puzzles. Inability to develop a plan and to carry it out suggests the possibility of inadequate frontal lobe function in some cases.

Learning disabilities tend to occur in varying degrees. To test for the existence of a "true" disability versus a "pseudo-disability," Luria taught children how to do the test items that they failed. On retesting a short time later, he found that some children still could not do the test items and had "true" disabilities. The remainder of the children divided into two groups. One group improved greatly, and the other group scored about midway between the nonimprovers and the best group (pseudo-disabled) (the editors).

FRONTAL LOBES AND PLANNING

This author has described disturbances in the completion of certain programs in patients with severe lesions of the frontal lobes. Even greater defects may be observed in most complex forms of behavior when the patients have to develop their own strategies and to construct their own plan and programs. This can be seen in experiments where the patients have to elaborate on some operations in order to single out decisive points of information.

Several years ago Sokolov proposed a special technique for analyzing such perceptive strategies. This was followed with experiments by Arana on normal subjects and by Tikhomirov on patients with lesions of the frontal lobes. A subject whose eyes are closed receives two sets of checkers placed in forms of the letters H or E. He has to touch them successively with his finger and recognize which letter is presented to him. In the first stages, the subject's search for information is of an extended type; he touches all checkers, but he soon develops a special strategy to single out only those points of information that are decisive for the discrimination of both letters. In the last stage, one trial is sufficient for accomplishing this task.

No such process of the development of a strategy is observed in patients with lesions of the frontal lobes. As a rule, such patients touch all checkers, but they do not use the information they receive nor do they shorten their search. The act of touching successive checkers is not used for preliminary orientation to the given pattern, and the patient's "conclusion" is a mere guess.

A similar breakdown of complex strategies of perceptive search is observed in experiments using the observation of pictures and simultaneous recording of the subject's eye movements. A normal subject is shown a complex thematic picture, for example, a well known picture of the outstanding Russian painter, Repin, "The Unexpected Return." It presents a man who unexpectedly returned home after he had spent many years in a Tsarist prison. Fastened to the subject's sclera is a little mirror that reflects a beam of light to a photosensitive paper and records the subject's eye movements. After recording the subject's free observation of the picture, he is asked some questions, such as, "How old are the members of the family?" "How are they dressed?" "Is the family rich or poor?" "How long was the man in prison?" Records of the eye movements made during 3 minutes show how complex the exploratory activity of a normal subject is and how profoundly the structure of his search changes, depending upon different instructions (Yarbuss, 1967).

No such complex structure of the search is observed in patients with severe lesions of the frontal lobes. These patients do not exhibit any strategy in their search behavior; they do not make any attempts to single out the decisive information by comparing separate details of the picture. They fix on some points of the picture, sometimes chosen at random, and their eye movements have a chaotic or perseverative character; no change of ocular movements manifests itself when different instructions are given. It becomes evident that no active strategy of search is applied by these patients and that their perceptive behavior has become profoundly changed.

May it be assumed that the structure of active forms of behavior is severely disturbed as a result of lesions of the frontal lobes? This author has had many occasions to prove the correctness of this assumption in a long series of experiments with different kinds of intellectual activities. In all cases, he came to the conclusion that the *human frontal lobes are intimately involved in the realization of complex strategies of behavior and that severe injuries of these parts of the brain result in a breakdown of the basic structures of their intellectual activities* (Luria and Homskaya, 1966*).

CONCLUSIONS AND PERSPECTIVES

This author fully agrees with the assumption that the human central nervous system is really a "conceptual nervous system" and that its basic task consists in elaborating some inner codes that result in the execution of certain plans and programs and in the regulation and control of man's behavior. This makes the human brain an organ of freedom.

It is likewise known that the origin of the highest form of self-regulating behavior does not lie in the depths of the organism, and, in order to disclose its roots, one has to turn to the complex forms of a child's relations with his social environment and to his acquisition of language. Some features of the dramatic history of this development are already known, and there is some basic data concerning its cerebral organization. It is now evident what an important role the frontal lobes of the human brain play in the organization of the conscious control of behavior and that a profound breakdown of this highest from of self-regulated activity is observed in severe lesions of this wonderful part of the brain.

However, after much research, this author has to admit that research is only at the very beginning and that unsolved problems many times exceed the scope of present knowledge. The neurophysiological mechanisms of the highest forms of conscious regulation of behavior are not yet known, nor is the intimate physiological mechanisms of the work of the frontal lobes yet known. Knowledge of the frontal lobes is still too vague. Only during recent years have researchers begun to acquire some data concerning their complex functional organization.

Thus, researchers are still very far from the solution to the basic problem—the neuropsychological organization of man's conscious action—and they can only look forward with envy and hope to the work of the next generation of psychologists who will one day take our place and bring to a successful conclusion the work now only started.

LITERATURE CITED

Calanchini, P. R., and Trout, S. S. 1971. The neurology of learning disabilities. In: L. Tarnopol (ed.), Learning Disorders in Children: Diagnosis, Medication, Education. Little, Brown, Boston.

French, J. D., Herhandes, P. R., and Livingston, R. B. 1955. Projection from cortex to cephalic brain stem reticular formation in monkey. J. Neurophys. 18.

Hebb, D. O. 1955. Drives and the CNS (conceptual nervous system). Psych. Rev. 62(4).

Hebb, D. O. 1965. The evolution of the mind. Proc. Roy. Soc. B. 161.

Homskaya, E. D. 1970. Brain and Activation. Moscow University Press, Moscow.

Jasper, H. H. 1959. Functional Properties of the thalamic reticular formation. In: Brain Mechanisms and Consciousness. Oxford University Press, Oxford.

Lindsley, D. 1960. Attention, consciousness, sleep and wakefulness. Handbook of Physiology, Vol. III.

Livanov, M. N., Gavrilova, N. A., and Aslanov, A. S. 1966. Correlation of bio-potentials in human frontal lobes. In: A. R. Luria and E. D. Homskaya (eds.), Frontal Lobes and Regulation of Psychological Processes. Moscow University Press, Moscow.

Luria, A. R. 1961. The Role of Speech in the Regulation of Normal and Abnormal Behavior. Pergamon Press, Oxford.

Luria, A. R. 1963. Restoration of Brain Functions after War Trauma. Pergamon Press, Oxford.

Luria, A. R. 1966. Higher Cortical Functions in Man. Basic Books, New York.

Luria, A. R., Blinkov, S. M., Homskaya, E. D., and Critchley, M. 1967. Impairment selectivity of mental processes in association with lesions of the frontal lobes. Neuropsychologia 5.

Magoun, H. W. 1958. The Waking Brain. Charles C Thomas, Springfield, Ill.

Moruzzi, J. 1954. The psychiological properties of the brain reticular formation. In: Brain Mechanisms and Consciousness. Oxford University Press, Oxford.

Nauta, W. I. 1958. Hippocampal projections and related nervous pathways to the midbrain of the cat. Brain 81.

Nauta, W. I. 1964. Some efferent connections of the prefrontal cortex in the monkey. In: I. M. Warren and K. Akert (eds.), The Frontal Granular Cortex and Behavior. McGraw-Hill, New York.

Pribram, K. H. 1959. On the neurology of thinking. Behavioral Sciences.

Walter, W. G. 1953. The Living Brain. W. W. Norton, New York.

Yarbuss, A. L. 1967. Eye Movement in Visual Perception. Plenum Press, New York.

Chapter 3

Evoked Potentials and Learning Disabilities

James R. Evans

Imagine a test instrument that promised the following: 30-minute administration time, objective machine scoring, relative culture fairness, usefulness at all ages, and cost within reason. Suppose this test could provide: evidence for existence and nature of brain dysfunction, a sensitive indication of basic neurological response to remedial techniques, information concerning sense modalities most efficient for learning, favorite cognitive styles, likelihood of responsiveness to medication for hyperkinesis, and presence and nature of any intersensory integration or attentional deficits.

Such an instrument does not appear to be outside the realm of possibility in the near future. At present, researchers at several centers in the United States using elaborate equipment requiring highly specialized knowledge are reporting the accomplishment of such measures. They are employing a relatively new technique most commonly referred to by the terms cortical evoked response, or evoked potential (EP). There is good reason to believe that within the next few years these procedures will be perfected and will become widely available for clinical use.

NEED FOR A TEST OF NEUROLOGICAL DYSFUNCTION

In the early years of the learning disabilities movement, the notion was prevalent that many, if not all, learning-disabled persons suffered from some subtle, deviant malfunction of the central nervous system (CNS) (Clements, 1966). Many still assume such dysfunctions to be the basic cause of specific learning disabilities. However, it is often stated that there are no valid means of determining the existence of such defects and no definite remedial implications even if they could be determined. That view is justified on the grounds that traditional neurological and electroencephalographic (EEG) evaluations rarely have proved useful for individual diagnosis of subtle brain dysfunction, and only a few remedial approaches use procedures based on specific neurological-type examination data (e.g., those of Ayres (1972) and Delacato (1963)). Thus, the majority of today's teachers of learning-disabled children appear to consider the behavioral aspects of learning disorders more relevant than the neurological aspects.

Reliable diagnosis of specific and relevant neurophysiological disabilities could be of great benefit in the area of learning disabilities. The presence and nature of CNS dysfunction could prove to be more delimiting and precise and, in the long run, provide more educationally useful criteria than presently used psychometric tests of vaguely defined psychological processes. Neurophysiological-type measures could be used in conjunction with psychoeducational tests to enable more precise delineation of subtypes of learning disabilities; this, of course, could have implications for differential treatment approaches.

NATURE OF EVOKED POTENTIALS

Traditional EEG measures are rather crude indicators of ongoing electrical activity at points on and near the surface of the outer portions (cortex) of the brain under the scalp sites at which electrodes have been attached. By amplifying the tiny electrical signals from these sites, one can make a record of them on continuously moving paper. This graphic record of electrical activity during specified time periods is referred to as the electroencephalogram, or EEG. Frequency (in cycles per second (cps), or Hertz (Hz)) and amplitude (voltage, roughly comparable to power) characteristics of these signals at the various sites provide useful information regarding tumors and convulsive disorders, such as epilepsy, and indicate states such as sleep and coma.

The evoked potential (EP) technique also involves brain electrical activity, but it is concerned with brain response to some distinct event in contrast to a passive recording of on-going global brain electrical activity. Thus, if a living organism with intact sensory systems and cortex is subjected to a flash of light, or a tachistoscopically presented word, or a click, this stimulus will bring about (evoke) a change in brain electrical activity that can be detected in the EEG. This event-related brain response involves the creation of temporary differences in polarity or in degree of polarity within brain areas. Such differences can be measured in volts as electrical potential and constitute the *evoked potential*.

The first responses to a sensory stimulus usually are greatest in areas of the cortex with the most nerve cells specialized for processing the particular type of stimulus involved, e.g., the occipital area for a visual stimulus. (See Figure 1 for an idealized visual representation of an EP and its course over time.) Aspects of the EP that most often differ among persons and diagnostic categories include the amplitudes of various peaks on the EP waveform and the time (latency) in thousandths of a second (milliseconds, or msec) from onset of the stimulus to the various peaks or to points where the wave form crosses a zero voltage baseline (horizontal axis). Amplitude refers to distance above and below a baseline and usually is in terms of millionths of a volt (microvolts, or μV). The term "peak" refers to the various high and low points on the waveform. Peaks above the baseline traditionally, but not invariably, are referred to as negative peaks and those below the baseline as positive peaks. Aspects of the EP during approximately the first 50 msec generally are labeled "early components," while those from 150 to 500 or 600 msec are known as "late components."

Although the response evoked by a single discrete stimulus is represented in the EEG, it will be so embedded within the other (ongoing) brain electrical activity that it is difficult or impossible to detect. Because of this, 50 to 100 or more discrete (unvarying) stimuli commonly are presented at rates of about one per second. Brain electrical activity immediately following each stimulus is recorded and eventually summed by a computer across the many stimulus presentations. The brain response to each of the unvarying stimuli causes approximately the same pattern of changes in polarity for each presentation, while the background activity varies randomly during the same time period. Thus, the evoked responses should sum to a grand total that is much larger than the total of the background activity. Background activity will tend, in part, to cancel out (average out) (Figure 1). Because of this the EP measures most often used are referred to as averaged evoked responses or *averaged evoked potentials* (AEPs).

Method of Evoked Potential Measurement

AEP measurement involves decisions regarding: 1) nature of the stimuli to be presented, e.g., sense modality, intensity, duration, interstimulus interval, number, and order of presentations; 2) cortical areas and corresponding scalp electrode sites from which potentials are to be recorded; 3) aspects of the AEP to be measured, e.g., overall amplitude, amplitude at specified times after onset of stimulus, variability of the AEP, time (latency) to specified points on the AEP waveform (an example of the latter could be the positive peak at the 300 msec point, which is often referred to as P 300 or P 3); 4) EEG frequencies that will be involved in the EP measure, e.g.,

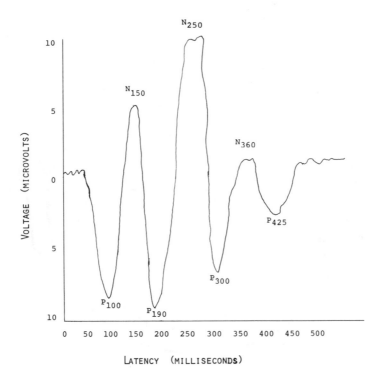

Figure 1. Example of a visual EP recorded from the occipital area with light flashes as stimuli. Peaks above the zero voltage baseline are negative, while those below (troughs) are positive. The peaks are labeled N for negative and P for positive followed by the latency in msec.

some investigators filter out frequencies above 40 cps; 5) rate of sampling of the EEG by the computer (every 5 msec is a common rate).

Scalp electrode placement usually follows the International 10-20 System (Jasper, 1958). These electrode locations are shown in Figure 2. Although this system specifies 19 electrode sites, it is uncommon to use them all in any one investigation. Some commonly used scalp sites are occipital (O_1, O_2), parietal (P_3, P_4), central (C_3, C_z, C_4), and frontal (F_3, F_4). The odd-numbered subscripts refer to the left side, the even-numbered to the right side, and the subscript z refers to the midline.

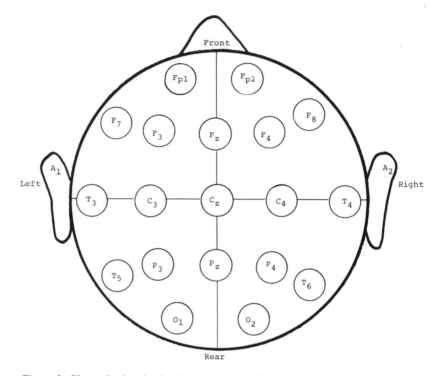

Figure 2. Electrode sites in the International 10-20 System. F, frontal; P, parietal; T, temporal; O, occipital; z, center line. Odd numbers are on the left hemisphere, and even numbers are on the right hemisphere.

Thus, scalp site O_1 is over the left occipital area, and C_z is on the midline over the central area of the cortex. Each electrode must be referenced (grounded) to some other area. Commonly used reference sites are C_z, ear lobes, and forehead.

Usually, the subject is seated comfortably in a reclining chair in an electrically shielded, quiet room with dimmed lights. Electrodes are attached and he is given directions to try to relax and attend to the stimuli that subsequently will be presented. Stimulus presentation usually is controlled by a computer program, and often some means is used to ensure that the subject is, in fact, attending. For example, a few dim flashes may be interspersed with the brighter ones, and he is to count the former by operating a hand-held counter. The time required for an AEP evaluation will, of course, vary widely with the number of samples taken, types of stimuli presented, etc. Ordinarily, however, no more than 10 to 20 minutes of data-gathering is done. Reliability is not increased much with further sampling, and the amount of data collected with longer times via a computer becomes so large as to be impractical.

Reviews of the many and rapidly growing uses of the AEP with humans, as well as more detailed descriptions of the technique, can be found in texts by Callaway (1975), Regan (1972), and Shagass (1972). Although the AEP technique has been used successfully in research and clinical work in several areas of disability, e.g., deafness, visual defect, and emotional disturbance, its use with learning-disabled persons and hyperkinetic children is emphasized in this chapter.

REVIEW OF RESEARCH ON LEARNING DISABILITIES

One of the earliest published investigations involving computer-scored aspects of the EEG and learning disabilities was that of Ertl and Douglass (1970). Using equipment known as a Neural Efficiency Analyzer (NEA) to measure visual evoked response (VER) latency in both cerebral hemispheres, these investigators reported significantly above-average right to left absolute differences among a group of nine persons suffering from "primary reading disabilities." Latency in this study was average time, following stimulus presentation, to second and third baseline (zero voltage point) crossings of the EP waveform. Very few details regarding subjects and method were given.

Subsequent use of the NEA for diagnosis of learning disabilities has yielded conflicting findings. Ertl (1975) in a research newsletter reported that an investigator (Dr. Gregory Walsh) at the University of California at Los Angeles Medical School was able to identify correctly 95 percent of 100 subjects diagnosed as having minimal brain dysfunction (MBD) during "blind" testing of 100 normal children and 100 MBD cases.

His method involved use of the absolute difference score in msec between right and left hemispheres, with scores of 10 or less usually characterizing the normal group and those greater than 10 nearly always present in the MBD group. No information was given concerning ages or other characteristics of subjects, or how many normals also had scores above 10. In a later study, Evans, Martin, and Hatchette (1976) were unable to differentiate any of three presumed subtypes of learning-disabled children either from each other or from a group of 13 academically gifted or a group of 13 normally achieving children using NEA absolute difference scores. However, in this study the various groups were not matched on age or IQ, and age has been found to be correlated with NEA scores.

Conners (1971) reported results of four studies of averaged VERs in children with reading disabilities. In all cases electrodes were placed at left occipital (O_1), right occipital (O_2), left parietal (P_3), and right parietal (P_4) and referenced to center midline (C_z). Light flashes were used as stimuli. For his first study an 11-year-old boy with a severe reading disorder and five other members of his family were evaluated. EPs from each site were normal in the mother, who had no reading problems. On the other hand, each of the five family members who had a reading disability had similar abnormal flattening in the negative component (N_{200} about 200 msec) of the left parietal (P_3) VER waveform (Figure 3). Because the father and his four children had similar abnormalities, this may be considered evidence for a genetic-neurological basis of a reading disorder.

Twenty-seven third- and fourth-grade children with reading and other learning disabilities were subjects in the second study. Correlation coefficients of -0.61 and -0.64 were obtained between absolute voltage level (raw μV) of the same late component of the left parietal (P_3) VER and reading and spelling levels, respectively, at time of beginning a summer remedial reading program. Achievement was measured with the

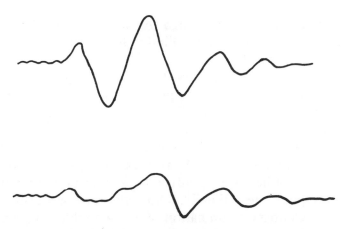

Figure 3. Genetic brain-wave abnormality and reading disability. A father and his four children with reading disabilities all had the same brain-wave abnormality in the visual evoked response of the left parietal lobe. Brain-wave responses from the other areas were normal. The mother's brain-wave responses were all normal, as was her reading ability. Top curve is typical normal brain-wave response from the left and right occipital lobes and the right parietal lobe. Bottom curve is typical abnormal left parietal response. (Reprinted with permission from Tarnopol and Tarnopol, 1976 (after Conners, 1971).)

Wide Range Achievement Test. No significant relationships were found at other electrode sites.

In the third of Conners' studies, 10 relatively good readers were matched with 10 very poor readers on age, IQ, and social class. All subjects were males from a school for learning-disabled children. Mean age was 11.9 years. Again a correlation of -0.63 was found between achievement (learning quotient) and the late component of the left parietal VER, but with no other electrode sites. Conners concluded that good readers apparently have more negativity in certain aspects of the left parietal VER.

In his final study of this series, Conners used 26 learning-disabled children of similar age and with average level full-scale IQs. Half of them had relatively high verbal and low performance IQs and half had the opposite verbal-performance pattern. The two groups were matched on age and sex. Neurological status also was evaluated for each, and the high verbal-low performance group was found to be significantly more impaired neurologically.

In the low verbal-high performance group, the VER amplitude of another wave (large positive wave at about 140 msec, P_{140}) was found to be significantly greater (more positive) at left and right parietal and right occipital sites. In the high verbal-low performance (more impaired neurologically) group, the latency of the late (200 msec, N_{200}) negative component referred to earlier was significantly slower at both left and right occipital sites. Finally, although not specifically mentioned by Conners, examination of his data tables suggests that both good readers and high verbal IQ children, as groups, show less variability in amplitude of the 140 msec P_{140} positive component in the left parietal area.

Conners' results were supported in a more recent investigation by Preston, Guthrie, and Childs (1974). Using light flashes and tachistoscopically presented words as stimuli for the VER, they evaluated nine 9-year-old disabled readers of average IQ, a control group matched on age and IQ, and another control group matched with the experimental group on reading level and IQ. Electrode placement was P_3, P_4, O_1, O_2, and C_z. Absolute deviation (positive or negative) from the zero reference line of the pen recorder at 180 and 600 msec after stimulus onset was recorded. Only the measurements from P_3 were reported. The reading-disabled group showed significantly lower amplitudes than either control group at 180 msec but not at 600 msec. This effect was significant for flashes but not for words. The authors concluded that the findings indicate a general (not specific to reading) neurophysiological deficit in some disabled readers. They feel that this may well be centered in the left angular gyrus area (approximately left parietal, or P_3) of the cortex. They did, however, mention that attentional factors possibly could account for the observed differences, and they suggested additional research to resolve this question.

Shields (1973) studied evoked responses of 10 children with disabilities in the processing of visual stimuli and 10 normally learning children matched on age, sex, handedness, verbal IQ, and socioeconomic status. All subjects were of average or above-average IQ (range 95 to 135), and their ages ranged from 10 to 13. Electrodes were placed over "corresponding scalp locations in the central area of each cerebral hemisphere" (apparently C_3 and C_4) and at O_1 and O_2. Light flashes, pictures, designs, words, and nonsense words were used as stimuli. Evoked responses were quantified by measuring amplitude and latency of "five basic peaks" in the wave form. Seven of the ten measures significantly separated the two groups: latency to each peak was longer, and amplitudes of the first and third positive peaks were greater in the learning-disabled group. Shields felt her results suggested that learning-disabled children may have relatively immature brain responses (require longer time to process information) and may have to focus more attention than others in order to process stimuli.

The published research on AEPs and learning disabilities is summarized in Table 1. These investigations have opened an entire new area to research and have provided evidence of usefulness of the AEP as a diagnostic tool. Now there is a need to replicate them and to expand them to include subjects of different ages, races, and learning styles with varying types of learning disabilities. Until there have been successful replications, most will be open to the criticism that significant findings resulted from the fact that many measurements were taken and some statistically significant ones, therefore, would have been expected because of chance alone.

Future researchers need to control carefully the variables of reading disability, age, sex, handedness, and attention. The nature of reading disability probably varies with age (Satz, Rardin, and Ross, 1971), and normal AEPs change significantly from year to year during development (John, personal communication). Electrophysiological differences between the sexes and between right- and left-handed persons have been

Table 1. Summary of AEP research on learning disabilities

Investigators	Subjects	Measures	Main findings
Ertl and Douglass (1970)	9 children with "primary" reading disability	Hemispheric differences in visual EP; light flashes used as stimuli	Greater right-left hemisphere latency differences in a learning-disabled group
Walsh (in Ertl, 1975)	100 normal and 100 MBD children	Same as above	Greater right-left hemisphere latency differences in the MBD group
Evans, Martin, and Hatchette (1976)	64 learning-disabled, 13 normal, and 13 gifted children	Similar to above	No significant latency differences among groups
Conners (1971) (1)	6 members of a family, 5 of whom had reading disability	Visual EP amplitude and latency with light flashes as stimuli; electrode sites O_1, O_2, P_3, P_4, C_z	Attenuation of 200 msec (N_{200}) negative component of P_3 (left parietal) EP in the poor readers; genetic left parietal dysfunction
Conners (1971) (2)	27 third- and fourth-grade learning-disabled children	Same as above	Significant correlations (-0.61, -0.64) between achievement and voltage of N_{200} component of left parietal EP
Conners (1971) (3)	10 good readers matched with 10 poor readers	Same as above	Correlation of -0.63 between same variables as above

Conners (1971) (4)	26 learning-disabled children, half with low verbal (V)-high performance (P) IQs and half vice versa	Same as above	Low V-high P subjects had higher amplitudes of P_{140} at P_3, P_4, and O_2; latency of N_{200} longer at O_1 and O_2 in high V-low P group
Preston, Guthrie, and Childs (1974)	Nine 9-year-old poor readers matched with 9 others on age and IQ and matched with 9 on reading level and IQ	Visual EP amplitude with light flashes and words as stimuli	Lower EP amplitude at 180 msec at left parietal among poor readers with flashes used as stimuli
Shields (1973)	10 with visual processing disabilities matched with normally learning subjects	Visual EP amplitude and latency with light flashes, words, designs, and pictures as stimuli	Longer latencies to each of 5 EP peaks, and higher amplitudes of 2 peaks in the learning-disabled group (peaks not specified)

reported (Dimond and Beaumont, 1974). Callaway (1975) implies that attentional disturbances can significantly modify AEPs independently of other neurophysiological dysfunction. Finally, there is a need to consider that the subjective emotional value of a stimulus affects one's AEP characteristics. Thus, for example, if words were used as stimuli, poor readers who consider the written word to be an aversive stimulus might show abnormal AEPs at least in part because of this, rather than some more basic, unlearned, neurophysiological dysfunction.

Despite weaknesses in the AEP vs. learning disabilities research to date, there seems to be sufficient evidence to indicate that a basic neurophysiological abnormality exists among some learning-disabled children. For example, many children with reading disorders show abnormal visual AEPs to light flash stimuli over the left parietal (P_3, angular gyrus) area of the cortex.

HYPERKINETIC BEHAVIOR IN CHILDREN

Several researchers have used AEP techniques in studies of the hyperkinetic syndrome. This syndrome typically is characterized by motor overactivity, inability to concentrate, short attention span, difficulty in inhibiting responses, low levels of frustration tolerance, irritability, and explosiveness. Perceptual and cognitive dysfunctions and specific learning disabilities are also commonly observed in conjunction with this syndrome.

The majority of relevant AEP studies have attempted to relate differential clinical drug responses in normal and hyperkinetic children to AEP differences and in most cases have demonstrated some unique relationships. One of the earlier and better known studies was that of Satterfield et al. (1972). Auditory AEPs to clicks presented at two speeds were recorded from the vertex (C_z) area of five male hyperkinetic children who responded well to methylphenidate hydrochloride (Ritalin).

These AEPs were compared to those of five children who did not respond well and to those of 11 normal controls. All groups were matched on age, IQ, and sex. IQ scores were within the normal range, and the subjects averaged 7 years of age. The study was of the "double blind" type, i.e., neither subjects nor raters knew which children were administered Ritalin and which received a placebo. Subjects were off drugs for at least 3 weeks before pretesting, and the drug group was on Ritalin for a 3-week period before post-testing. Dosage varied; it was adjusted weekly for each child until a good response was obtained or side effects occurred. Hyperkinetic best responders to Ritalin had higher pretreatment auditory AEP amplitudes at P_{60}, N_{120}, P_{180}, and N_{280} and lower recovery of AEP amplitude than worst responders. Recovery rate apparently was based on comparison of AEPs to clicks presented at faster versus slower rates. After drug treatment, the best responders' AEP amplitudes decreased, while those of the worst responders and the placebo group increased. The authors felt their results supported a view of low CNS arousal in children who benefit most from stimulant medications such as Ritalin.

Conners (1972) discussed general features of some of his research on responses to medication of children with behavioral and learning disorders. Various psychoeducational test and EEG measures, including amplitudes and latencies of visual and auditory AEPs to flashes and clicks, were obtained for a total of 71 children with severe behavioral and/or academic problems. Subjects' average age was 9.5 years. The study was a double blind type comparing three groups on effects of Ritalin, dextroamphetamine sulfate (Dexedrine), and a placebo. Pre- and post-drug measures were separated by 1 month. AEP measures of basic subject groups were compared, as were those of subtypes of subjects determined from a factor analysis of pretreatment psychoeducational test scores and gain scores.

Major findings included decreased visual AEP latencies at

P_{180} and N_{240} in the two drug groups. There were no other general, global drug effects reported; however, significant (not specified) drug-related AEP amplitude and latency changes were found for some subtypes of subjects, including changes in hemispheric dominance relationships. Conners stresses the need for researchers and clinicians to consider subsets of learning-disabled and hyperactive children. By lumping all children together in a supposedly homogeneous group, treatment effects occurring for some but not for all may be obscured in the overall group results.

Twenty-four children between 6 and 12 years of age with IQ scores above 80 and diagnosed as having MBD and 48 normal children matched on age served as subjects in a study by Buchsbaum and Wender (1973). These investigators noted that earlier work with normal adults had demonstrated that amphetamines both function as stimulants and cause abnormal rates of increase in amplitude of AEPs with increasing stimulus intensities. They reasoned that children with whom these drugs have the paradoxical effect of decreasing hyperactivity should be those who, before drug treatment, show the highest rates of AEP amplitude increases with stimulus intensity increases and whose rates of increase become normalized when on medication. By contrast, nonresponders should show the normal adult behavioral and AEP responses while on the medication. Visual and auditory AEP amplitude and latency measures were based on four different intensities of light flashes, on flashes of light modulated by 10-cps waves, and on 60-decibel (db) tones presented at half-second intervals. MBD subjects had been on stimulant medication for at least 1 month before the study; half were taken off medication 3 to 6 days before the AEP measures in order to obtain "off medication" scores. Four to eight months later all were retested.

As expected, when on amphetamines, drug responders showed a decrease and nonresponders an increase in rate of visual AEP amplitude increase with greater stimulus intensities. This was significant at N_{140} and P_{200}. The MBD group under the four intensities of visual stimulation had larger off-drug, peak to trough amplitudes for the N_{140}—P_{200} component of the EP waveform, faster rates of amplitude increase with stimulus intensity increases, and shorter latencies at P_{100} and P_{200} than the normal control group. This group also showed greater variability (greater immaturity) of the auditory AEP than the normal group. Normals' visual AEP latencies at P_{200} decreased with increasing stimulus intensity, while those of the MBD group increased. Other findings regarding comparison of drug responders with nonresponders and/or normals were as follows: P_{100}, N_{140}, and P_{200} latencies in the four intensity visual stimulus conditions decreased with intensity increases in the responders when on drugs, while the opposite occurred with the nonresponders. Responders, off drugs, showed a lower-than-normal decrease in latency at P_{200} with increased stimulus intensity. AEPs to the sine wave modulated light increased in amplitude with age in responders but decreased with age in the normal group. Finally, hemispheric asymmetry of AEPs increased with age in responders but decreased in the normal group.

Buchsbaum and Wender considered this a preliminary study that needs replication under double blind conditions with a placebo group and a longer medication free period before off-drug testing. They did, however, believe their AEP results provided evidence that many MBD children are more immature, have more attentional deficits than age- and sex-matched controls, and may show increased motoric activity because of hypoarousal and "sensory underload." Presumably, such children are those who respond to stimulant drugs.

Most of the earlier AEP research on hyperkinesis involved responses evoked by simple stimuli such as clicks under conditions of passive attention, i.e., the child was given directions simply to listen to or observe the stimuli. At least two more recent investigations have considered AEPs of hyperkinetic children under conditions of active attention. The fact that the unique behavioral characteristics of hyperkinetic children are most often reported in situations requiring focused attention suggests that AEPs taken under conditions of active attention should be more discriminating than those obtained under conditions of passive attention.

Halliday et al. (1976) conducted a two-part study in which visual and auditory AEPs were measured under conditions of both passive and active attention. An electrode was attached at C_z and referenced to linked ears. In the active condition, subjects were told to press a switch when they observed any of several dim flashes interspersed among a larger number of bright ones. Correct detections were worth 25 cents each. The principal purpose of the research was to determine if AEP measures given before a clinical trial of Ritalin could differentiate hyperactive children who subsequently respond to the drug from those who do not.

In the first part of the study, 17 white hyperactive boys (average age, 9 years) with IQs ranging between 91 and 121 served as subjects. In the second part of the experiment, subjects were 20 male and 5 female hyperactive children averaging 9 years of age and with IQs from 68 to 138. Pretest AEP measures were taken at an initial session. At two later sessions, each subject received either a 10-mg Ritalin capsule or a placebo 45 to 60 minutes before AEP recordings. After the third session, all children were placed on 10 mg of Ritalin twice daily, and dosage was adjusted until either an optimum clinical response or side effects occurred. After 2 weeks of stabilized dosage, each subject's behavior while on Ritalin and while on a placebo was rated by teachers and parents. Finally, at the end of the school year, each child's progress was rated by his pediatrician as either greatly improved (responders), or slightly improved, or not improved (nonresponders). All ratings were done in a double blind manner.

In the active attention condition, responders had smaller N_{145}—P_{190} visual AEP amplitudes off drug (on placebo) and showed increases when taking Ritalin. In contrast, nonresponders showed slight decreases. The authors felt that these findings were evidence for a normalizing effect (increased amplitude) of Ritalin upon the attentional responses of some hyperactive children (responders) and an abnormal effect upon those of others (nonresponders).

A recently completed study reported by Prichep, Sutton, and Hakerem (1976) also involved auditory AEP measures taken under varying conditions of attention. AEP differences between hyperkinetic and normal children and the effects of Ritalin on AEPs of hyperkinetic children were investigated. Eight hyperactive boys were tested when on Ritalin and when on a placebo, and eight other hyperactive and eight normal boys were tested on a placebo. Subjects of the three groups were matched on age, and all had IQ scores above 80. Auditory AEPs from C_z (referenced to right ear) were recorded using single and double clicks as stimuli. Subjects were tested under two different sets of instructions: 1) certainty condition in which they were told before a trial whether a single or double click would be presented (low attentional demand), and 2) uncertainty condition in which they had to guess whether a single or double click would be presented (high attentional demand). Correct guesses were monetarily rewarded.

Effects of Ritalin were noted in comparison with changes in the hyperactive drug group between when on drug and when on placebo relative to changes in the hyperactive placebo group from test to retest. In the uncertainty (high-attention) condition, the drug appeared to have normalizing effects on the hyperactive group. The P_{186} component increased and the N_{250} component decreased in amplitude in the on-drug condition, thus becoming more nearly like the amplitudes of those components in the normal group.

The hyperkinetic placebo group was found to differ from the normal group in having larger amplitude of the P_{295} component of the AEP to the second click in the certainty condition. Prichep, Sutton, and Hakerem (1976) suggest this may reflect an inappropriate responding to task demands inasmuch as higher amplitude would be expected only in the uncertainty (greater attentional demands) condition.

As with several other investigators, Prichep, Sutton, and Hakerem considered that their findings supported an attentional deficit-low arousal model for hyperkinesis. They cautioned that their findings support only a task-specific hypo-arousal, i.e., only under high-attention conditions.

A summary of the studies on AEPs and hyperkinesis in children discussed above is provided in Table 2.

Although the results of AEP research with hyperkinetic children are not entirely consistent, they have provided evidence of electrophysiological differences between hyperactive and normal children, as well as between hyperactive children who respond to stimulant medications and those who do not. Furthermore, it is now known that differential neurophysiological responses are associated with different responses to stimulant drugs. For example, the AEPs of children who respond well to medication tend to become more like those of normal children. Some clinical use of these findings now seems warranted.

Finally, the rather consistent finding of AEP characteristics in a high percentage of hyperactive children, which are commensurate with immaturity, poor attentional control, and/or hypoarousal of the CNS, provides strong support to the maturational lag, attentional deficit, and hypoarousal theories of hyperkinesis.

POTENTIAL APPLICATIONS

The research just described shows that AEP differences exist between groups with various learning or behavioral disabilities and control groups. Replication of these studies could validate AEPs as useful and unique diagnostic tools. The AEP procedure, however, has potential for contributing far more than simple diagnosis of the presence of CNS dysfunction, high risk for a future learning disability, or likelihood of responsivity to medication. Research is needed to determine its usefulness in the detailed diagnosis of the basic nature of individual learning disorders.

Localization of Brain Dysfunction

Conners (1971) and Preston, Guthrie, and Childs (1974) provided evidence implicating the left parietal area of the cortex in some types of reading disorders. Because this area also has been found at autopsy to be damaged in some cases of acquired dyslexia after head injuries or cerebral vascular accidents in adults, it seems rather certain that damage or other defect in the left angular gyrus is a basic cause of some reading disabilities.

Walsh's findings, as reported by Ertl (1975), suggested that hemispheric asymmetry of AEP latency characterizes many children with behavior control problems and associated learning difficulties. This supports the notion that some abnormality of left-right cerebral hemisphere interrelationship underlies many learning disorders. Reading difficulties frequently have been attributed to inadequate hemispheric control or dominance (Delacato, 1963; Orton, 1937).

Recently there has been increasing speculation on the role of the corpus callosum in control of interhemispheric relationships (Geschwind, 1965). The corpus callosum is a large nerve fiber that serves as the primary connection between the right and left hemispheres. Measures of corpus callosum integrity might prove useful in investigations of the nature of learning disabilities. Such measurement is possible using AEPs in conjunction with unilaterally presented visual or tactual stimuli.

In summary, investigations designed to discover specific areas of dysfunction should prove useful in furthering the theoretical understanding of brain-behavior relationships and may well have practical value in delineating subtypes of learning-disabled children.

Table 2. Summary of AEP research on hyperkinesis in children

Investigators	Subjects	Measures	Main findings
Satterfield et al. (1972)	31 hyperkinetic boys and 23 normal controls; for most EP aspects of study subjects were 11 hyperkinetics and 11 normals matched on age, IQ, and sex	Amplitude of auditory EPs to clicks (various other EEG measures also taken); electrode sites approximately C_3, C_4, ipsilateral ear	Hyperkinetic responders to Ritalin showed higher pre-treatment auditory EP amplitude at P_{60}, N_{120}, P_{180}, and N_{280}, and lower recovery of EP amplitude than worst responders; on-drug, best responders' EP amplitude decreased, while those of worst responders and placebo group increased; concluded, children who benefit from stimulants have low CNS arousal
Conners (1972)	71 children with severe behavioral and/or academic problems at home or school	Amplitudes and latencies of visual and auditory EPs to flashes and clicks; electrode sites O_1, O_2, P_3, P_4, C_z	Amphetamine and Ritalin groups had decreased visual EP latencies at P_{180} and N_{240}, but placebo group did not; significant (but not specified) drug-related EP amplitude and latency changes for some subtypes

Buchsbaum and Wender (1973)

24 MBD children and 48 normals matched on age; ages 6 to 12 yrs; IQs above 80

EP amplitude and latency; stimuli were tones, flashes of varying intensity, and flashes modulated to varying degrees by sine waves; electrode sites C_z, right ear; O_1, O_2, ipsilateral ear

MBD group off-drug had larger amplitude to light flashes at N_{140}—P_{200}, faster rates of amplitude increase and increased P_{200} latency with increases in stimulus intensity, shorter latencies at P_{100} and P_{200}, and greater auditory EP variability than did normals. Drug responders, off-drug, showed below-normal decreases of latency at P_{200} with increased stimulus intensity; on drugs, responders showed a decrease and nonresponders an increase in both latencies and rate of amplitude increase with increased intensity at N_{140} and P_{200}; hemispheric asymmetry increased with age in responders and

Continued

Table 2. *Continued.*

Investigators	Subjects	Measures	Main findings
			decreased in normals; concluded MBD children are more immature, have more attentional deficits than controls, may be because of hypoarousal
Halliday et al. (1976)	Experiment I: 17 white hyperactive boys; experiment II: 25 hyperactive children; 20 boys, 5 girls, 4 black, 21 Caucasian	Experiment I and II: visual and auditory EP variability and peak to peak amplitude under conditions of passive and active attention: stimuli were flashes and clicks; electrode sites C_z and linked ears	Nonresponders to Ritalin on drug showed less visual EP variability in the passive than in the attention condition; responders had smaller N_{145}—P_{190} visual EP amplitude off-drug and showed increases with Ritalin under conditions of attention; concluded, Ritalin normalizes attentional responses of hyperactives
Prichep, Sutton, and Hakerem (1976)	8 hyperkinetic children tested under Ritalin and a placebo, 8 hyperkinetic children tested twice under placebo, and 8 normal controls tested twice under placebo	Auditory EP amplitude under 2 conditions of attention: certainty and uncertainty of stimulus; stimuli were single and double clicks; electrode sites C_z, right ear	Hyperkinetic placebo group had greater amplitude at P_{295} to second click in certainty condition, smaller positive and larger negative components at P_{186} and N_{250} in uncertainty condition, and

less differences between responses under certainty and uncertainty conditions at P_{186} than did normals; hyperkinetic children when on drugs had: a) larger N_{130} and smaller P_{186} and P_{295} amplitude to first click in uncertainty condition; b) increased P_{186} and decreased N_{250} amplitudes; c) greater uncertainty to certainty conditions differences; concluded, hypoarousal of hyperkinetic children leads to attentional deficit only under conditions demanding great attention; Ritalin had normalizing effect

Integrity of Basic Psychological Processes

The most common definition of children with learning disabilities specifies that they "exhibit a disorder in one or more of the basic psychological processes involved in understanding or in using spoken or written language." AEP procedures should be useful in the study of these processes.

Probably no symptom is reported more often among learning-disabled children than some difficulty with attention. These children much of the time are unable to direct and maintain attention toward stimuli relevant to problem solving. They often seem unable selectively to inhibit responses to irrelevant external and internal cues, and/or to refocus attention to different cues when needed for a specific learning task. In other words, they appear to be distractible and/or perseverative. It is believed that these behaviors result from a condition of hypoarousal (Wender, 1971) affecting various aspects of attention. Others have emphasized only the defects in active attention, i.e., in voluntarily directing and maintaining attention.

Because it seems most likely that the specific nature of attentional disorders in learning-disabled children varies with individuals, some objective means of investigating this is desirable. Several characteristics of AEPs seem especially relevant. When a sufficiently strong or new stimulus is initially presented, a rather elementary form of attention known as an "orienting reaction" occurs. This consists of events such as turning the head toward the stimulus, changes in respiration rate and blood flow, inhibition of cortical alpha rhythm in the EEG, and, of special relevance here, an increase in the amplitude of the early components of EPs in response to the stimulus. With continued presentation of the stimulus, these reactions are inhibited and disappear, a process referred to as "habituation." The reactions will, however, recur if discriminable changes are made in the stimulus. These facts suggest use of AEP measures to determine the stimulus thresholds necessary for attracting attention as well as to investigate other aspects of attentional disorders. For example, abnormally long periods required for habituation could reflect a defect in one's inhibitory mechanisms, including the ability to inhibit irrelevant stimuli.

The late components of AEPs are of larger amplitude when the stimulus is relevant and attended to actively than when it is irrelevant. In many AEP studies, mobilization of this active (as opposed to passive) attention is attempted by requiring the subject to count the occasional unique stimuli, e.g., dim flashes in a series of many bright ones. The comparison of late components of EPs to designated relevant and irrelevant stimuli might provide valuable information concerning the presence, form, and extent of any disturbances of active attention.

Intersensory integration (sometimes referred to as cross modality matching or coordination of schemas) also seems amenable to evaluation with the AEP technique and is a process often implicated in learning disorders. Masterson (1975) reports that AEPs to compound stimuli such as simultaneous presentations of a flash and click, or flash, click, and tactile stimulus normally are of greater amplitude than AEPs to single modality stimuli. Thus, it should be possible to gain insight into the sensory integration process in any learning-disabled person by comparing single modality AEPs to those obtained using various types of compound stimuli.

Within the past decade much has been written concerning the various cognitive styles of individuals, methods of measuring them, and modification of teaching techniques to accomodate the different styles. Among the most commonly discussed of these styles are field dependence and field independence.[1] There is now evidence (Guyer and Friedman, 1975)

---

[1] The rod and frame test may be used to determine "field articulation." The subject is required to align a rod vertically in the center of a tilted frame that distorts the visual field, with no other visual cues. Those who are able to ignore the tilted frame and align the rod fairly well are considered "field independent." They appear to be analytic in cognitive tasks. "Field dependent" subjects make more errors in setting the rod vertically because they are unable to ignore the distorting effects of the frame. They are said to respond to the total field and tend to use a less verbal, more global, way of processing information (the editors).

that a high percentage of learning-disabled boys function basically with a field-dependent style and that this style is mediated primarily by the left hemisphere (Cohen, Berent, and Silverman, 1973). AEP techniques should prove useful as a supplementary method of determining the presence of this cognitive style.

Measures of Response to Treatment

As noted, AEPs have been demonstrated to be useful as sensitive measures of the response of hyperactive children to medication. In the case of hyperactivity, however, behavioral responses to medication usually are rather obvious and rapid, and the need for a neurophysiological measure perhaps is not as great as with other learning disabilities. Evaluation of the responses of learning-disabled children to remedial approaches (e.g., perceptual-motor training, behavior modification, vision training) typically involves pre- and post-testing of academic achievement separated by a time period of several months. It is assumed that at least that much time is required before any basic neurophysiological changes are manifest at the level of observable behavior such as reading or writing. Great savings in time and increased precision in remedial approaches could be realized if a sensitive measure of change in neurophysiological processes relevant to potential for academic achievement were available. AEP measures appear to be especially promising for this purpose. For example, poor readers receiving remedial assistance could be monitored for increase, or lack of it, in amplitude of the N_{200} (200 msec negative) component of the visual AEP in the left parietal area. Conners (1972) has noted changes in this AEP component among some children receiving Ritalin; however, this seems to be the only published report of an application of AEP techniques to the measurement of the response to treatment for learning disorders.

Research in Progress

Laboratories at several universities are actively engaged in investigation of the EP correlates of reading and other learning disabilities. The most advanced and comprehensive of these research programs appears to be that of Dr. E. Roy John of the New York Medical College's Brain Research Laboratory. Dr. John and associates have administered their Quantitative Electrophysiological Battery (QB) to thousands of children and adults and claim to be able to detect not only the presence of brain dysfunction but also, in many cases, specific aspects of a learning disorder such as attentional disorders, short-term memory defects, and modality-specific disorders of information processing (Goleman, 1976). The QB involves computer-scored measures of ongoing EEGs as well as AEPs, and it requires 15 minutes' administration time. Nineteen electrode sites are involved, and scores on a total of 85,000 "test" items are obtained for each child. John estimates that the cost of a QB examination in the future will be as low as 15 dollars. He believes that such examinations eventually may provide valuable information regarding brain dysfunction in infants as young as 2 days old.

The present author recently conducted AEP research with reading-disabled children in the laboratories of Dr. Enoch Callaway at the Langley Porter Neuropsychiatric Institute in San Francisco. Specifically, an attempt was made to replicate certain of Conners' (1971) results. The research also was designed to test the hypothesis that reading-disabled children with other evidence of auditory-visual integration difficulties will show abnormal AEPs over the left angular gyrus area (P_3) to compound auditory-visual stimuli. Data presently are being analyzed. Dr. A. Salamy at Sonoma State Hospital, California, is investigating hemispheric differences and interhemispheric transfer in reading-disabled children using visual and tactile AEPs. Drs. Lewis and Rimland (San Diego Naval Base) are using visual AEPs in attempting to discriminate between Navy recruits who respond to a regular remedial reading program and those who do not.

Dr. Malcolm Price and associates at The Johns Hopkins University are continuing their AEP research with reading-disabled persons and have expanded their interests to include adults with reading disorders. Undoubtedly other investigators are presently active in this area, but the above-mentioned ones are best known to this author.

CONCLUSIONS

AEP measures have proven highly useful in many areas, and there is rapidly increasing evidence of their value in the fields of diagnosis and remediation of learning disabilities. Although they are perhaps more culture-fair than most of the psycho-educational tests used today in that there is little or no verbal communication required of the subject and minimal examiner influence on his responses, AEPs are not culture-free; brain structure can be influenced by environment (Callaway, 1975).

Much more research is needed, and there seems especially to be a need for some coordination of efforts among researchers. The number of different electrode sites that might be involved, the almost infinite number of possible variations in stimuli that can be used to elicit AEPs, and the several types of AEP measures that can be calculated are only a few of the reasons why comparisons of findings of different researchers is difficult. Some coordination among leading researchers could minimize these problems.

EP measures appear to be an area with major possibilities for both theoretical and practical advances in the learning disabilities field. Perhaps the day is not far distant when all children will be screened with a neurophysiological test battery and divided into remediation-relevant groups on the basis of brain organization. Perhaps remediation for some will consist, in part, of EEG biofeedback training to help develop a cerebral organization pattern more consistent with academic readiness. And perhaps the new breed of labeling that is likely to accompany this would even prove beneficial. The pendulum swings.

ACKNOWLEDGMENTS

The author gratefully acknowledges the assistance of Enoch Callaway, III, M.D., of the Langley Porter Neuropsychiatric Institute in San Francisco, California, in preparation of the portion of this chapter describing characteristics and measurement of evoked potentials.

LITERATURE CITED

Ayres, A. J. 1972. Sensory Integration and Learning Disorders. Western Psychological Services, Los Angeles.

Buchsbaum, M., and Wender, P. 1973. Average evoked responses in normal and minimally brain dysfunctioned children treated with amphetamine. Arch. Gen. Psych. 29:764–770.

Callaway, E. 1975. Brain Electrical Potentials and Individual Psychological Differences. Grune & Stratton, New York.

Clements, S. D. 1966. Minimal Brain Dysfunction in Children. NINDB Monograph No. 3. Department of Health, Education, and Welfare, Washington, D.C.

Cohen, B. D., Berent, S., and Silverman, A. J. 1973. Field-dependence and lateralization of function in the human brain. Arch. Gen. Psych. 28:165–167.

Conners, C. K. 1971. Cortical visual evoked response in children with learning disorders. Psychophysiology 7:418–428.

Conners, C. K. 1972. Stimulant drugs and cortical evoked responses in learning and behavior disorders in children. In: W. L. Smith (ed.), Drugs, Development, and Cerebral Function, pp. 179–199. Charles C Thomas, Springfield, Ill.

Delacato, C. H. 1963. The Diagnosis and Treatment of Speech and Reading Problems. Charles C Thomas, Springfield, Ill.

Dimond, S. J., and Beaumont, J. G. (eds.). 1974. Hemisphere Function in the Human Brain. Elek., London.

Ertl, J. 1975. Research Newsletter No. 1. Neural Models Limited, Toronto.

Ertl, J., and Douglass, V. 1970. Evoked Potentials and Dyslexia. Neural Models Limited, Toronto.

Evans, J. R., Martin, D., and Hatchette, R. 1976. Neural Efficiency

Analyzer scores of reading disabled, normally reading, and academically gifted children. Percept. Mot. Skills 43:1248–1250.

Geschwind, N. 1965. Disconnection syndrome in animals and man. Brain 88:237–294.

Goleman, D. 1976. A new computer test of the brain. Psych. Today 9:44–48.

Guyer, P. L., and Friedman, M. P. 1975. Hemispheric processing and cognitive styles in learning-disabled and normal children. Child Dev. 46:658–668.

Halliday, R., Rosenthal, J., Naylor, H., and Callaway, E. 1976. VER predictors of clinical response to methylphenidate in hyperactive children: An initial study and replication. Psychophysiology. In press.

Jasper, H. H. 1958. The ten-twenty electrode system of the International federation of societies for electroencephalography and clinical neurophysiology. Electroenceph. Clin. Neurophys. 10: 371–375.

Masterson, R. B. 1975. The method of compound stimuli for the assessment of cortical integration. In: J. W. Prescott, M. Read, and D. Coursin (eds.), Brain Function and Malnutrition, pp. 373–380. John Wiley & Sons, New York.

Orton, S. 1937. Reading, Writing, and Speech Problems in Children. W. W. Norton, New York.

Preston, M., Guthrie, J. T., and Childs, B. 1974. Visual evoked responses in normal and disabled readers. Psychophysiology 11: 452–457.

Prichep, L. S., Sutton, S., and Hakerem, G. 1976. Evoked potentials in hyperkinetic and normal children under certainty and uncertainty: A placebo and methylphenidate study. Psychophysiology. In press.

Regan, D. 1972. Evoked Potentials in Psychology, Sensory Physiology and Clinical Medicine. Wiley-Interscience, New York.

Satterfield, J., Cantwell, D. P., Lesser, L. I., and Podosin, R. L. 1972. Physiological studies of the hyperkinetic. Am. J. Psych. 128:1418–1424.

Satz, P., Rardin, D., and Ross, J. 1971. An evaluation of a theory of specific developmental dyslexia. Child Dev. 42:2009–2021.

Shagass, C. 1972. Evoked Brain Potentials in Psychiatry. Plenum Press, New York.

Shields, D. 1973. Brain responses to stimuli in disorders of information processing. J. Learn. Disab. 6:501–505.

Tarnopol, L., and Tarnopol, M. 1976. Reading and learning disabilities in the United States (with emphasis on California). In: Lester Tarnopol and Muriel Tarnopol (eds.), Reading Disabilities: An International Perspective, pp. 287–325. University Park Press, Baltimore.

Wender, P. 1971. Minimal Brain Dysfunction in Children. John Wiley & Sons, New York.

Chapter 4

Application of Neuropsychological Principles in the Diagnosis of Learning Disabilities

Lawrence C. Hartlage
and
Patricia L. Hartlage

There is little disagreement that diagnosis, or evaluation, of a problem is a logical first step in determining an appropriate treatment or remediation of that problem. This is as relevant in psychoeducational assessment and remediation as it is in any other professional field.

The process of learning depends to a considerable extent on the functioning of the central nervous system (CNS). Disabilities in acquiring educational skills often reflect dysfunctions of the CNS structures that subserve the acquisition of these skills. To better comprehend the nature of a child's failure to profit from academic instruction, it often helps if his learning dysfunction can be related to the underlying neurological substrates of that dysfunction.

Unfortunately, most training programs for teachers and psychologists take place in settings where there is no course in the field of brain-behavior relationships to make relevant

111

neurological and/or neuropsychological information an integral part of the training. As a result, many clinicians working with learning-disabled children are left with such a lack of understanding of brain-behavior relationships that, in cases where specific neurological dysfunction is made obvious by their test or observational evaluation, they are forced to conclude their diagnostic statements to the effect that "this child appears to be suffering from some form of brain damage."

Diagnostic conclusions such as "brain damage" or "minimal cerebral dysfunction" are too broad to relate to any meaningful prescription. For a more useful differential diagnosis, consider the following:

1. The brain is divided longitudinally into two cerebral hemispheres, damage to either of which can result in quite different types of problems
2. Each cerebral hemisphere is grossly divided into four lobes, and damage to a specific lobe may result in a different type of dysfunction
3. In addition to highly specialized areas of function in the cortex, the brain contains numerous pathways that connect these cortical areas with each other and carry incoming sensory information and outgoing motor commands to and from the cortex
4. The brain contains millions of neurons, and disabilities in learning may reflect the number of neurons that are damaged as well as their location
5. Acute and chronic brain dysfunction exert strikingly different influences on the nature of the brain-behavior relationship
6. While the brain cannot replace a neuron once it is lost, the remaining intact neurons may be able to take over the functions of the damaged cells or in some degree to compensate for their loss

It is most important in prescribing a remedial approach for a given deficit to assess what the brain can do as well as what it cannot do, and it is especially important to determine the brain's ability to process the information involved in the proposed remedial approach.

For at least the past 100 years, it has been known that the brain is much more complex than a simple on-off mechanism that can be usefully described as either "damaged" or "normal." Broca, for example, first identified a center that appeared to be specifically related to expressive speech, and other neurologists subsequently described other brain areas whose integrity was apparently necessary for specific mental operations, such as visual memory and writing.

Although these discoveries of fairly discrete, specific brain-behavior relationships helped to clarify the dependency of certain higher mental functions on the integrity of the appropriate underlying brain areas subserving such functions, these early findings were not related to any variables of concern to school psychologists until the latter half of this century by the work of Halstead at the University of Chicago. Reitan, a student of Halstead's, developed and refined the field of clinical neuropsychology in assessing brain-behavior relationships, and he is probably the legitimate father of the practice of neuropsychology today. In 1955, Reitan published a landmark paper on the differential effects on intellectual functions of lesions found on different sides of the brain (Reitan, 1955). Since that time, a prodigious amount of research relative to correlates of lateralized brain dysfunction (e.g., Kløve 1959; Luria, 1965; Reitan, 1964; Reitan and Tarshes, 1959), chronic versus acute brain dysfunction (e.g., Fitzhugh, Fitzhugh, and Reitan, 1961, 1962, 1963), and a wide range of related phenomena has appeared in the literature and provides school psychologists with a fund of information of consequence for psychodiagnostic activities.

NEUROPSYCHOLOGICAL
IMPLICATIONS OF COMMON PSYCHOMETRIC TESTS

Although it is possible to do a relatively precise job of assessing and describing the condition of the brain by means of specialized neuropsychological test instruments and procedures, for most school psychologists the time involved in the development of sufficient diagnostic and interpretive expertise, combined with the comparatively long period of time required to administer and interpret formal neuropsychological test instruments, makes the use of such instruments and procedures impractical for everyday use in school psychological practice. Furthermore, the specifications of which brain areas are dysfunctional, the etiology, and the probable duration of the dysfunction are not questions typically brought to learning-disability clinicians. On the other hand, psychometric instruments in relatively common use among such clinicians do provide the basis for some evaluation of the functional integrity of the brain.

Test Correlates of
Right and Left Cerebral Hemisphere Dysfunction

Because the left hemisphere subserves language and related functions (Figure 1), its integrity is reflected by a large number of common psychometric instruments. One might expect to find, for example, in a child with left-hemisphere dysfunction a significantly lower Verbal than Performance IQ on the Wechsler Intelligence Scales. Reading and spelling achievement tests, auditory discrimination and comprehension tests, and picture vocabulary tests all reflect the integrity of the functions of the left hemisphere. Some instruments (e.g., the Wepman Test of Auditory Discrimination and subtests of the Illinois Test of Psycholinguistic Abilities) assess specific components of language, while others (e.g., the Gates, McGinity, and Durrell oral and silent reading tests) assess the integration of multiple language skills, such as auditory, visual, receptive, associative, and expressive skills.

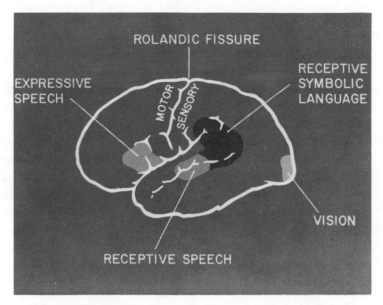

Figure 1. Gross localization of function in the left cerebral hemisphere.

Conversely, dysfunctions in the right hemisphere are likely to manifest themselves in tests that deal with spatially related tasks (e.g., Performance subtests of the Wechsler Scales, Bender Visual Motor Gestalt Test, and Benton Visual Retention Test) but may be comparatively unreflected on language-related tests. However, caution is required when drawing inferences of right-hemisphere dysfunction. The largest and most vulnerable neurons in the brain are those that control motor function. It is not unusual to observe severe motor handicaps with normal or even superior intellectual ability in persons with cerebral palsy. Failure to recognize this selective vulnerability of motor neurons can lead to misinterpretations of psychometric test data, especially in drawing conclusions about whether brain dysfunction is lateralized or diffuse. While damage to the right hemisphere typically depresses the Wechsler Performance IQ, a similar depression may result from bilateral motor impairment from old diffuse insults, fatigue, tranquilizing drugs, depression, or, in a right-handed person, even from an insult to the parts of the left hemisphere that control the motor function of the right hand.

In general, psychometric tests that compare the functional symmetry of the right and left cerebral hemispheres help to obviate the *false positive errors* (i.e., diagnosing a condition as being present when it is not) that may result from using arbitrary cutting scores below which CNS dysfunction is presumed. Such tests may also control for the *false negative errors* (i.e., diagnosing a condition as absent when it is present) that can occur when a person with lateralized dysfunction has an overall score on some criterion measure sufficiently high to cause him to be classified as falling within the normal range.

Test Correlates of the Localization and Extent of Brain Dysfunction

The identification of a lateralized dysfunction is a valuable piece of information in plotting remedial strategy, for instance, in recommending an emphasis on either verbal or nonverbal teaching methods. More precise localization of areas of brain impairment further enhances the value of the psychodiagnostic process in predicting which remedial techniques will be successful. While poor performance on a spatially related task such as the Bender Visual Motor Gestalt Test may be useful in confirming right-hemisphere damage suggested by other psychometric instruments, it may become more useful in localization and hence in remedial planning when the cause of the poor performance is more carefully scrutinized.

There are at least three possible contributors to poor performance on the Bender Test: impaired visuoperceptual input, impaired perceptual-motor output, or impaired associational functions involving the translation of visual input into motor output. (Limiting the possible components of impaired performance to only these three assumes that generalized intellectual subnormality, emotional disturbance, poor effort, etc., have already been ruled out and the alternatives have been narrowed down to factors involving the CNS.) After completion of the test, the clinician may select two or three of a child's worst reproductions and ask him if they are like or different from the original designs. If he responds, for example, that his reproductions are different from the original and he identifies how they are different, visual-perceptual dysfunction may be excluded. If he can further explain what corrections are needed to improve his reproduction, an associational deficit may also be excluded. If, despite this knowledge, he is still unable to improve his reproductions on repeated attempts, one can reasonably conclude that his dysfunction is localized in the motor cortex of the brain. Further localization of the motor disability, i.e., right, left, or bilateral, can be ascertained by simple timed motor tests, (e.g., peg boards) with comparison of the "dexterity" of the right and left hands. Because of the selective vulnerability of motor neurons, in most cases, one finds bilateral impairment. In contrast, the child whose poor Bender performance stems from an inability to perceive the visual stimulus accurately suffers from a posterior or sensory dysfunction in the right hemisphere and presents a more serious and challenging problem for remedial strategies.

While a few of the Wechsler subtests reflect reasonably localized functions, (e.g., Picture Completion and Digit Span reflect posterior right- and left-hemisphere abilities, respectively), the majority of common psychometric test items are impure and of little localizing value. It is possible, however, by careful attention to the specific difficulty a child encounters in performing a task and by generating a few successive sieve hypotheses concerning general brain areas involved, to make some valid conclusions about localization of dysfunctions. For example, is this problem diffuse or localized? If localized, is it more anterior (motor) or posterior (sensory)? If it is posterior, is it more left hemisphere (verbal) or right hemisphere (spatial)?

The findings may be put together in a topographical

map of apparently intact and impaired areas of brain function. By using standard scores of tests reflecting different functions, areas of impairment can be graded as to the severity of their dysfunction.

Test Correlates of Chronicity of Brain Dysfunction

In most situations encountered by school psychologists, the vast majority of children manifesting CNS dysfunction will be reflecting chronic damage or genetic differences. Acute disorders, whether resulting from trauma, neoplastic diseases, intracranial bleeding, or other causes, will typically be referred to and managed by medical specialists, with school psychologists involved only occasionally to help determine the extent of these medical problems on the child's mental functioning. It is of value, however, for the school psychologist to have some general knowledge of differentiating acute from chronic brain disorder, both to refer the case to the appropriate medical specialists and to estimate the feasibility of suggested educational programs.

One important difference commonly found between chronic and acute lateralized CNS dysfunction, as reflected in psychometric test scores, is the magnitude of the discrepancy between the levels of functioning on tasks subserved by the two cerebral hemispheres. Large discrepancies between verbal and performance IQ levels are much more commonly found in acute lateralized disorders, although the absence of a large discrepancy does not necessarily rule out a problem of recent onset. Similarly, if all Wechsler subtests are fairly uniformly depressed, the likelihood of acute disorders is less than in cases where either individual subtests or clusters of subtests are substantially lower than the rest.

Valuable information relative to the differentiation of chronic and acute disorders can often be obtained from constellations of abilities that might reasonably be expected to be similar. For example, if a child's evaluation results in a Verbal IQ in the borderline retarded range, with his Performance IQ in the low normal range, and his reading test levels in essentially the normal range, there is reason to wonder how a child with a borderline retarded Verbal IQ acquired such competence in reading. This raises the question of possible deterioration of intellectual skills after the reading skills had been acquired. It is generally true that older, acquired skills tend to be more resistant to loss than are more recently acquired information or skills, and it is not uncommon for a patient with a neurological problem of recent onset to forget recent events much more readily than he forgets older, learned facts. Somewhat analogous is a progressively senile adult who can remember events, addresses, phone numbers, and facts from long ago but forgets where he left his keys or his car. Similarly, a patient with an acute neurological disorder whose fund of knowledge is still intact may not be able to learn or to remember new material or to master new problem-solving sets.

Because of this tendency in acute neurological disorder for new types or applications of learning to be more severely affected than older knowledge, performance tests that reflect abilities to form new associations and to maintain sustained attention may be more sensitive to acute brain disorders than are verbal tests that measure the patient's fund of general information or word knowledge. Tests such as the Shipley Institute for Living Scale (Shipley, 1940), which compare word knowledge with new problem-solving sets and express the relationship in terms of a conceptual quotient, are thus likely to be fairly effective in detecting acute types of disorders, although their discriminant utility for more chronic types of disorders is likely to be less impressive.

A problem involved in using screening types of instruments such as the Shipley-Hartford or the Wechsler Hold–Don't Hold configural scoring approach (which compares the patient's scores on subtests presumably resistant to loss with his scores on subtests presumably more likely to reflect sudden decline) for detecting acute brain disorders is their tendency toward a fairly high false-positive rate. This occurs because such discrepancy scores can also result in the classification of acutely psychotic, schizophrenic, or depressed patients as "organic." Furthermore, it is not uncommon for screening types of tests to be misused by translating the findings based on one population to another without questioning the assumptions involved in determining the original cutting scores. The Trail-Making Test, for example, involves a comparison of the patient's performance on simple sequencing versus a double alternating sequencing task and has been found to differentiate organically impaired from normal subjects in a neurological or neurosurgical clinic population (Reitan, 1971). This test has been applied to a mixed population of psychiatric and neurologically impaired patients and found to be of little value in differential diagnosis between these two groups (Lacks et al., 1970). Considering the possibility of false-positive errors when using this instrument with a mixed psychiatric population, it is probably more meaningful to question its use in such a setting than to question its diagnostic validity. These apparently contradictory results illustrate the problems involved in the uncritical applications of neurological screening test cutting scores as an arbitrary index of acute dysfunction.

One source of information that may be overlooked in the differentiation of acute and chronic neurological disorders involves any changes in the person's typical life style, level of functioning, or emotional stability. Not uncommonly, acute brain disorders may be mistaken for psychiatric episodes. Irritability and lethargy, for example, may precede other symptoms of brain tumor. In cases of degenerative brain disease, progressive decline in academic functioning may be the earliest sign. Any case involving a sudden and inadequately explained change in behavior is much more likely to be associated with acute as opposed to chronic brain disorders, although other factors can and often may be involved.

Test Implications for Remedial Strategies

Although probably requiring considerably more sophistication in planning and execution than their use for gross diagnostic purposes, neuropsychological approaches to planning remedial strategies for educating children with chronic neurological handicaps offer tremendous potential to school psychology. If the pattern of a person's strengths and weaknesses resulting from CNS dysfunction can be accurately assessed, it is possible to develop appropriate remedial approaches.

In many cases, attempts at remediation that focus on diagnostic patterns of a child's weaknesses may be doomed to failure if the remedial strategies depend upon functionally impaired brain tissue. Programs involving many perceptual-motor, visual patterning, or neurological imprint methods, for example, may focus their main attention on developing specific abilities in cases where the underlying brain tissue necessary to support these abilities is damaged to the point where it cannot profit from this attention. For such cases, diagnosing an area of deficit and then building a remedial approach focused on the deficit area is not unlike determining that a child is unable to read because he is blind and then accelerating visual reading enrichment efforts.

In a child with serious impairment of the right parietal lobe, for example, one might reasonably expect to find evidence of a marked construction dyspraxia or inability to perform on tasks like the Wechsler Block Design subtest. Given such a deficit, it may be appropriate to avoid a great deal of emphasis on remedial printing or perceptual-motor design copying activities and to focus on using the intact verbal and symbolic functions of the left cerebral hemisphere to help the child bring his strengths to bear on learning. Similarly, just as one might use a tape recorder or listening comprehension approach to educate a blind child of average intellectual ability, without focusing on his deficit areas, it may be equally appropriate to use a similar approach in the education of a child who is dyslexic, or word blind, because of dysfunction in the posterior temporal areas of the dominant cerebral hemisphere.

A neuropsychological approach toward mapping the intact and dysfunctional areas of the brain may be used to indicate what is treatable and what will probably not respond to treatment. This may help to avoid a hit-or-miss approach toward remediating intellectual and/or academic problems secondary to injury to the brain and to develop individualized strategies for using the intact strengths in a given child.

SPECIALIZED TESTS

For comprehensive neuropsychological assessment, there is probably no better test battery than the one developed by Halstead and Reitan and subsequently refined and used by Reitan. In addition to a few fairly common psychometric instruments (e.g., Wechsler) it is comprised of an array of special instruments for the sensitive measurement of a wide variety of intellective, sensory, and motor abilities. In the hands of a trained and experienced neuropsychologist these tests have demonstrated impressive validity in detecting a range of types of brain disorders (Halstead, 1947; Reitan, 1971). Unfortunately, the level of skill involved in interpreting the results of this battery is such that there are few clinicians who can reliably produce meaningful interpretations. Consequently, relatively few centers are equipped and staffed to provide such comprehensive neuropsychological diagnostic support.

In some cases, clinicians have collected the various test instruments from the Reitan battery and have embarked on an optimistic and ambitious program aimed at duplicating Reitan's success. In many cases, the clinicians have either eventually discontinued their efforts and/or published results critical of the battery. In light of the repeated demonstrations of the diagnostic accuracy and validity of the battery in the hands of Reitan and his small group of trained researchers, one may conclude that the battery is valid when used by trained personnel.

There are two major approaches to the use of special

tests or diagnostic procedures in neuropsychological assessment. One approach, perhaps most commonly employed by clinicians with professional training in medicine, involves a successive-sieves type of strategy. Here the findings from one instrument or procedure dictate the next instrument or procedure to be used. A fairly common sequence in such an approach might involve physical observations for any structural, postural, muscular, behavioral, gait, or coordination anomalies. This would be followed by tests for any lateralizing signs of dysfunction, then for localizing signs, and perhaps finally assessments aimed at producing information relevant to the extent and type or cause of the dysfunction.

The more common approach used by researchers in brain-behavior relationships involves a fairly standard, comprehensive battery of tests and procedures that assess such diverse aspects of mental functioning as concept formation; measures of receptive sensory and integrative abilities involving visual, auditory, and tactile modalities; expressive language, motor, and integrative skills; memory for visual, auditory, and tactile stimuli; and intellective skills. With older children and adults, for example, a neuropsychological battery might typically include such measures as the Category Test, the Tactual Performance Test, the Time Sense Test, Speech Sounds Perception Test, Critical Flicker Frequency Fusion Tests, grip dynomometer, Finger Oscillation Test, Rhythm Test, the Trail-Making Test, Aphasia Screening Test, and an age-appropriate Wechsler Scale. A special battery has been developed for children ranging in age from 9 through 14 years (Reed, Reitan, and Kløve 1965), but comparatively little work has been done in the area of developing a comprehensive battery for very young children.

Although different clinicians might use slightly different combinations of tests, a fairly typical battery might include, in addition to the Wechsler, all or combinations of many measures of the following abilities:

1. Ability to identify a common principle in each of several groups of pictures (*Category Test*)
2. Rate at which stroboscopic flicker is seen as steady light (*Critical Flicker Frequency Fusion Test*)
3. Rate of completing a Sequin Formboard-type puzzle while blindfolded and subsequent ability to draw the board and its blocks from memory (*Tactual Performance Test*)
4. Ability to identify rhythmic patterns (*Rhythm Test*)
5. Identification of correct alternative from similar sounding nonsense words (*Speech Sounds Perception Test*)
6. Rate of rapid finger tapping (*Finger Oscillation Test*)
7. Ability to estimate time (*Time Sense Test*)
8. Ability to name common objects, letters, and numbers, identify body parts and sides, write, calculate, and understand spoken language (*Aphasia Screening Test*)
9. Rate of completion of simple visual sequencing task and rate of completion of a double alternation sequencing task (*Trail-Making Test*)
10. Ability to perceive paired tactile, auditory, and visual bilateral stimuli presented simultaneously (*Bilateral Sensory Stimulation Tests*)
11. Identification of which individual fingers have been slightly touched on their dorsal surface (*Tactile Finger Recognition Test*)
12. Identification of which numbers or symbols have been written on fingertips, without visual cues (*Finger Tip Number Writing Test*)
13. Ability to identify common coins by touch alone (*Tactile Form Recognition Test*)

Because many of the measures included in a fairly typical neuropsychological battery involve some sort of specialized apparatus and considerable complexities of administration and scoring, discussion is limited to two measures, one involving motor function and one involving sensory integration, to help illustrate how these subtests contribute to a meaningful diagnostic picture. A measure of fine motor dexterity, the Finger Tapping Test, requires the subject to tap as rapidly as possible with the index finger of each hand, with several trials given for each hand, resulting in a score representing the average number of taps per timed trial. To aid in accurate scoring, usually some counter with a standard resistance is used. A measure of sensory associative functioning is represented by the Finger Tip Number Writing Test, in which the subject is asked to report numbers written with a tapered rod on individual fingertips of each hand. An equivalent number of trials is presented to each hand, with visual cues not allowed so that identification must be made on the basis of tactile information.

Relationship between
Neurological and Neuropsychological Findings

In the development and evaluation of neuropsychological techniques for assessing various aspects of brain functioning, the results of neurological examinations or diagnostic conclusions are often used as criterion measures against which the validity of the neuropsychological findings are determined (e.g., Klatskin et al., 1972). Unfortunately, the two approaches involve somewhat different evaluative strategies and result in different kinds of data, so the use of one as a criterion against which the other is to be evaluated does not necessarily result in any direct measure of validity.

One approach to determining the relationship between the two involved having a child who had been referred for learning disability evaluation examined independently by appropriate neurological and neuropsychological procedures. Each examiner used the techniques of his specialty and made a tentative diagnosis based on his findings. Subsequently, both examiners would meet with specialists familiar with the child's educational and social history and with representatives from the speech, hearing, and reading specialists who had evaluated the child. All relevant data would be integrated and a comprehensive diagnosis reached. From a large number of children seen for comprehensive diagnostic evaluation, those cases involving equivocal or mixed diagnoses were dropped. Those cases having unequivocal diagnoses in one of three independent and non-overlapping categories (right-hemisphere abnormalities, left-hemisphere abnormalities, and diffuse abnormalities) were compared in terms of percent correct differential diagnostic accuracy. Because part of the neurological examination was based on a neurological history and part on a neurological examination, comparisons were run separately for history and examination as well as for combined neurological findings. The neuropsychological findings were in somewhat better accord with final diagnoses for children with lateralized CNS dysfunction, while the neurological examination findings were slightly better for children with diffuse CNS dysfunction. However, each approach identified the ultimate diagnosis at statistically significant levels in all diagnostic categories (Hartlage and Hartlage, 1973). In effect, these data suggest that the two approaches complement each other because each is somewhat more effective in detecting a different type of manifestation of CNS problem and so are probably best used in conjunction with rather than instead of each other (Table 1).

Of special interest in this study was the fact that the psychometric data, which was interpreted by a neuropsychologist, was based on standard psychometric instruments: the Wechsler Intelligence Scale for Children, Wide Range Achievement Test, Peabody Picture Vocabulary Test, Beery Developmental Forms Sequence, and Raven Progressive Matrices Test, supplemented by two brief items from the Halstead Battery, the Finger Oscillation and Finger Tip Number Writing Tests.

An approach sometimes considered to hold promise for assessing dimensions of brain-behavior relationships implements the electroencephalogram (EEG). Although its use is not common in school psychology evaluations, the EEG is sometimes considered to be an appropriate next step in the sequence of referrals resulting from suggestive findings in school psychological evaluations. To help clarify the relationship between the EEG and neuropsychological data, records of 111 patients who had both types of evaluations done within a 3- to 4-day period were analyzed. On the basis of the locus of EEG abnormality, records were sorted into categories of diffusely abnormal (N = 54), right-hemisphere abnormal (N = 14), left-hemisphere abnormal (N = 13), and normal (N = 30). Separate one-way analyses of variance were completed among groups on each of 18 measures of intellectual and academic ability levels converted to standard score equivalents. There were no significant differences among groups on any academic variables, and on the one intellectual variable, where the overall F ratio was significant, subsequent analyses of orthogonal components of variance suggested that this significant difference was probably artifactual (Hartlage and Green, 1971, 1972) (Table 2). Although the EEG is probably the diagnostic instrument of choice in determining possible seizure activity, it appears to be not nearly so sensitive as neuropsychological approaches in determining subtle, especially chronic, deficits involving intellectual or academic

Table 1. Percent correct differential diagnostic accuracy

	Diagnostic category (CNS dysfunction)		
Diagnostic procedure	Right hemisphere	Left hemisphere	Diffuse
Neurological examination	87[b]	77[a]	95[c]
Neurological history	80[a]	77[a]	75[a]
Combined neurological history and examination	87[b]	84[b]	95[c]
Neuropsychological evaluation	100[c]	92[b]	90[c]
Number of cases	15	13	20

[a] $p < 0.05$.
[b] $p < 0.01$.
[c] $p < 0.001$.

manifestations of CNS dysfunction (Hartlage and Green, 1973).

IMPORTANCE OF DEVELOPMENTAL FACTORS

Especially in younger children, for whom comprehensive neuropsychological instruments and procedures are not well developed and standardized, it may be necessary to depend to some extent on developmental manifestations of the symmetry of CNS maturation for diagnostic purposes. One fairly simple screening approach uses developmental milestones, comparing language with motor development, whereby six verbal and six motor milestones are measured at half-year intervals in the preschool child (Hartlage and Lucas, 1973a). Although such an approach lacks the precision required for any exact specification of the condition of a given brain area, it does provide a fairly reliable index of the relative developmental symmetry of the two cerebral hemispheres.

Perhaps of more importance, a careful recording of mental developmental milestones acquired by a child at given ages may contain information of considerable importance for helping differentiate chronic and acute manifestations at later ages. Consider a child, for example, whose Wechsler reveals a discrepancy of 18 points' superiority of Verbal over Performance IQ. If his developmental history indicates that he has consistently reached language developmental milestones at a comparatively earlier age than motor milestones, this may suggest a relatively chronic and presumably stable condition. Had his motor development consistently been accelerated over his language development, this discrepancy might represent a sudden decline in function and could be indicative of some acute right cerebral hemisphere problem.

The learning specialist must also be aware of the developmental process as it related to academic performance, i.e., a child at each age may rely upon different brain functions in the acquisition of a given academic skill. Reading

Table 2. Summary of analyses of variances among four EEG groups on intellectual and academic variables

Test	F ratio	Probability
Wechsler Intelligence Scale for Children		
Full Scale IQ	0.464	0.708
Verbal IQ	0.203	0.883
Performance IQ	0.025	0.602
Information	1.752	0.159
Comprehension	1.223	0.303
Arithmetic	1.585	0.196
Similarities	1.408	0.243
Vocabulary	1.041	0.376
Digit Span	1.240	0.298
Picture Completion	0.728	0.536
Block Design	1.480	0.222
Object Assembly	1.446	0.203
Coding	3.585	0.015[a]
Wide Range Achievement Test		
Reading	0.967	0.41
Spelling	0.344	0.79
Arithmetic	1.030	0.37

Based on the loci of EEG abnormalities, four groups were differentiated as follows: diffusely abnormal ($N = 54$); right hemisphere abnormal ($N = 14$); left hemisphere abnormal ($N = 13$); normal ($N = 30$).

[a] Based on analyses of orthogonal components of variance, this appears to be an artifact rather than a real difference.

ability, for example, depends much more heavily on visual information processing, especially processing dependent on visual sequencing, at early ages and gradually shifts to place greater reliance on auditory information processing by age 8 or 9. As a result, the inability of a beginning first-grader to make progress in the acquisition of initital reading skills may reflect developmental delay more specific to the right cerebral hemisphere, while reading problems in a third-grader may reflect problems involving the left hemisphere.

There is considerable interaction between a child's con-figuration of neuropsychological deficits and strengths and the academic instructional approach that will help him to optimize his ability to profit from instruction. Recent work relating configurations of ability and deficit patterns in 6-year-old children, for example, has shown that, for teaching initial reading skills, boys strongest in auditory sequencing might do better in a linguistic/phonic than in a special alphabet (Initial Teaching Alphabet, i.t.a.) or a look-say program. Conversely, girls strongest in integrating visual and auditory spatial stimuli would likely learn better in a traditional look-say curriculum than in a special alphabet curriculum (Hartlage and Lucas, 1973b). All 6-year-old children, regardless of sex, who possess good skills in both visual and auditory sequencing and in visual/auditory space skills, tend to learn best in an i.t.a. program (Hartlage, Lucas, and Main, 1972). With older children, these re-lationships tend to become progressively less stable, and by about age 8 or 9—or perhaps somewhat later in some learning-dis-abled children—have been replaced by other relationships appar-ently more dependent on left-hemisphere mediated strengths.

These findings might help to explain apparently contra-dictory findings, for example, that the Bender Gestalt per-formance has been found to be a good predictor of first-grade reading achievement (Keogh, 1969; Koppitz, 1970) but is of quite modest predictive value for reading accomplishment at age 7 or 8. Apparently the acquisition of early reading skills is somewhat more related to visuospatial functional integrity, while subsequent consolidation of reading and related lan-guage skills depends progressively less on right-hemisphere skills and increasingly more on the left-hemisphere symboli-cally mediated functions. For academic planning purposes, this suggests that although a child with chronic mild dysfunc-tion of the right cerebral hemisphere may be at considerable academic risk in beginning school years, greater reliance on comparatively intact left-hemisphere functions tends to offer an encouraging prognosis for subsequent educational accomplishment (Tarnopol and Tarnopol, 1976).

ILLUSTRATIVE CASES

A few illustrative cases may be of value in demonstrating neuropsychological test profiles associated with different types of problems related to underlying dysfunctional brain states.

Case I

Background   A 10-year, 2-month-old girl with previous good school and social adjustment has recently become whiney, tries to avoid going to school by making vague somatic complaints, and sometimes cries for no apparent reason during class. When handled firmly by the teacher, she can control her behavior in class, but the teacher is afraid that this girl is depressed and probably sufficiently emotionally disturbed to require psychological or psychiatric help. The teacher describes her as completely changed in the last 6 months.

The mother reports that the girl's development was pretty much like that of her older sister (age 13). She walked at 1 year and was using single words at approximately 12 months. She could throw a ball and spoke in phrases and short sentences at age 2. She had no serious childhood illnesses. Her mother was a bit vague about developmental milestones after age 2, because she had gone back to work and left the child with a babysitter. She mentioned that the girl had gotten good grades (mostly Bs) until this year. The mother dates the beginning of problems shortly after the death of the girl's grandmother, with whom the girl had been very close. The grandmother had lived with the family for the past 4 years and had "mothered" the girl considerably more than had the girl's mother. Since the grandmother's death, the girl has become quieter, preferring to be alone, and recently has begun crying at home when scolded for not doing her chores.

The school's immediate placement decision is whether or not to promote her to the fifth grade, because her work has been mostly Ds the last two grading periods. Psychometric testing was done, with the results shown in Table 3.

Discussion   The brief description of the girl's early mental developmental milestones suggests that her motor and language development were somewhat above average. Although there was some undoubted emotional trauma associated with the death of the grandmother, the fact that a girl with previously above-average verbal development earned a WISC Verbal IQ of 85 compared with a Performance IQ of 103 is sufficient to question the efficiency of her left cerebral hemisphere, not only in comparison with her right hemisphere but also with what is known about her previous verbal skills. The question of a possible recent change in efficiency of left cerebral hemisphere functioning is also raised by her sudden change in personality, recent drop in school grades, and patterns of the WISC Verbal subtests. Because the two Verbal subtests (Information and Vocabulary), which reflect her highest areas of performance, are also the areas of functioning that are least likely to be influenced by recent loss of functioning, there is strong evidence to support an hypothesis of recent onset of some sort of dysfunction with apparent greatest manifestation in the left hemisphere. Performance on the Bender and Draw-A-Person tests—both of which tend to reflect primarily right cerebral hemisphere integrity—are both within the normal range and are also compatible with the WISC Performance results. The Peabody test, reflecting old acquired verbal knowledge, is not likely to reflect any impairment, at least in the early stages of deterioration of functioning. The Raven Progressive Matrices, reflecting a combination of spatial problem-solving and linguistic mediation of problem-solving strategies, is predictably sensitive to CNS dysfunction and is comparatively impaired relative to most measures except the Verbal IQ scores. Wide Range Achievement Test scores, reflecting acquired knowledge accumulated over a period of time, do not show significant impairment other than that apparently little new knowledge has been acquired during the fourth grade. It is significant that on the Finger Tip Number Writing Test the preponderence of errors occur, on the right side, contralateral to the hemisphere with suspected dysfunction. Finally, the im-

Table 3. Summary of test data—Case I

Wechsler Intelligence Scales for Children
Verbal IQ 85, Performance IQ 103, Full Scale IQ 93

	Scaled score		Scaled score
Information	10	Picture completion	12
Comprehension	8	Picture Arrangement	10
Arithmetic	6	Block Design	12
Similarities	6	Object Assembly	11
Vocabulary	10	Coding	7
Digit Span	5		

Note: On the Wechsler subscales, the mean is 10 and the standard deviation is 3.

	Standard score
Bender Visual Motor Gestalt Test	97
Draw-A-Person	101
Peabody Picture Vocabulary Test	96
Raven Progressive Matrices	85

Wide Range Achievement Test	Grade equivalent	Standard score
Reading	4.2	93
Spelling	4.0	92
Arithmetic	4.4	95

Sensory: Finger Tip Number Writing (errors per 20 presentations)
    Right 7, Left 1
Motor: Finger Oscillation (taps per 10-second period)
    Right 29, Left 31.4

paired finger tapping speed of the preferred right hand, which in this case is actually somewhat slower than the nonpreferred left hand, supports less efficient functioning of the left cerebral hemisphere and also implicates motor as well as sensory association areas.

In general, this girl's case is fairly representative of a CNS problem of recent onset and of comparatively severe magnitude. She certainly ought to be referred for immediate neurological investigation.

Outcome   This girl was hospitalized for neurosurgical evaluation, and subsequently a tumor was removed from the left hemisphere. Following a brief convalescence, she was able to begin working on grade-appropriate tasks at home and reentered school 3 months postoperatively. Slightly more than 1 year after surgery, she was functioning at grade level without any significant learning deficits.

Case II

Background   An 8-year, 1-month-old boy who repeated kindergarten is referred for evaluation because of a concern that he may have to repeat first grade. He has trouble printing, often reverses letters, and is a very poor reader.

His mother reports that he knew his first and last names at age 3, copied a circle and rode a tricycle at age 4, could name money and copy an X at 4.5 years of age, and appeared to develop normally until he started kindergarten. After about 3 months of kindergarten, he began fighting with his classmates and had to be punished often for misbehaving. At the end of kindergarten he could define words such as *swing, orange,* and *eyelash* and could answer questions like, "Why do we wear shoes," but his teacher felt he was not ready for first grade and so he was retained. He did much better in his second year of kindergarten, but after a few months in first grade he again began having difficulties. He can read words like *come, father,* or *tree* but misreads easier words like *dog* or *was.* The teacher reports that he sometimes drops his books during class to create a disturbance and almost always comes back to class late after lunch hour. Sometimes he wanders around the halls at school instead of returning directly to the classroom from errands. The teacher thinks he is probably either emotionally disturbed or immature but does not want to fail him again because he does respond in class as though he understands the material, although the papers he hands in are messy, very poorly organized, and usually turned in last.

Medical   A pediatric neurologist examined the boy and reported a poor right-left orientation, poor time sense concept, dysdiadochokinesia (difficulty in rapid finger-thumb apposition) and mild choreoathetoid (tremor and writhing) movements on the left, construction dyspraxia (difficulty reproducing designs), and poor memory for figures, although memory for numbers was slightly better. She concluded that the child's academic difficulties probably result from minimal cerebral dysfunction. The results of the neurological examination are in agreement with the psychometric findings (Table 4).

Discussion   The developmental history of this boy reveals consistent manifestations of delayed development in general nonlanguage skills (e.g., 1-year delay copying a circle, riding a tricycle), compatible with his current comparatively lower Performance scores on the WISC. Both conditions indicate less efficient functioning of the right cerebral hemisphere, and the apparent persistence of the problem on a developmental basis suggests a chronic condition. His developmental history, for example, shows evidence that his verbal skills have always developed at approximately normal milestones, while nonlanguage skills have been delayed from 6 to 12 months since at least age 4. Classification of the child as having possible "MBD" would serve categorization requirements but be of little value in helping plan for the child's educational future. On the other hand, his educational future could be profitably developed around his comparatively intact left-hemisphere abilities, while demands for performance dependent on spatial integrative skills could be de-emphasized. A primarily verbal instructional approach, using linguistic reading cues rather than the spatial-configural cues involved in look-say initial reading instruction, would be one way of helping him maximize the application of his intact abilities to his learning. Similarly, it would probably be of help to lessen demands for neatly written papers, timed written assignments, and the like. He should be permitted to use verbal reporting to communicate his grasp of instructional material because his general verbal and language skills represent his best tools for learning and interacting with his environment.

Table 4. Summary of test data—Case II

Wechsler Intelligence Scale for Children
Verbal IQ 97, Performance IQ 79, Full Scale IQ 88

	Scaled score		Scaled score
Information	11	Picture Completion	8
Comprehension	12	Picture Arrangement	8
Arithmetic	8	Block Design	7
Similarities	9	Object Assembly	6
Vocabulary	10	Coding	6
Digit Span	7		

Note: On the Wechsler subscales, the mean is 10 and the standard deviation is 3.

	Standard score
Bender Visual Motor Gestalt Test	80
Draw-A-Person	83
Peabody Picture Vocabulary Test	104
Raven Progressive Matrices	75

Wide Range Achievement Test	Grade equivalent	Standard score
Reading	1.7	82
Spelling	1.4	79
Arithmetic	1.6	81

Sensory: Finger Tip Number Writing (errors per 20 presentations)
    Right 2, Left 5
Motor: Finger Oscillation (taps per 10-second period)
    Right 30.7, Left 24.1

The teacher's reports of this boy's behaviors and her interpretation of their meaning are fairly striking. Behaviors reflecting lack of coordination, such as dropping a book, are viewed as attempts to create a disturbance. The facts that he wanders the halls and comes to class late after lunch are viewed as indicative of his being immature or emotionally disturbed, rather than as possibly resulting from dysfunction of the CNS structures subserving the spatial orientation and time senses.

He may wander the halls, for example, because he forgets whether to turn left or right at a given corridor, or because he has no well integrated spatial concept of the way the school building is arranged. With this boy, as well as with the girl in Case I, it can be misleading as well as grossly unfair to the child to accept a simplistic "emotional disturbance" explanation of behaviors without first determining whether, in fact, the disordered behavior may result from cerebral dysfunction.

Outcome   Follow-up of this boy 2.5 years after the initial evaluation indicates that, by mid-fourth grade, he is functioning at an acceptable, though far from outstanding, level. By focusing more teaching emphasis on his comparatively intact language skills, coupled with the decreasing importance of spatial types of skills in later elementary grades, this boy is able to stay with his class and to function at a slightly below-average (C minus) level.

Case III

Background   An 8-year, 4-month-old boy with an academic history of average work and reportedly normal developmental milestones was involved in a summer playground accident in which he was struck in the head with a bat and sustained a skull fracture on the left side of his head. After 3.5 months, he seemed to have completely recovered from his injury and was considered medically capable of returning to school. He had completed second grade (B average) just before his accident and entered the third grade.

During his first few days back at school, his teacher reported that he seemed to be daydreaming, inattentive, and unmotivated. The parents were quite concerned about their possible role in this change in his behavior, because during his illness they had been extraordinarily solicitous in responding to all of his whishes and wondered if perhaps they had made him too dependent by their overprotectiveness.

Discussion   This boy's academic and school history suggest that before his accident he functioned at approximately high-normal levels. When his current psychometric scores are compared with his previously adequate school work, there is a strong suggestion that his current scores do not reflect his long-standing functional level (Table 5). It is most unlikely that, with the impairment reflected on his psychometric scores, he could have done adequate school work during his first 2 years of school. Although there is no consistent lateralizing pattern manifest in his psychometric scores, the areas of greatest dysfunction correlate fairly well with the pattern of his head trauma. There is maximal impairment of left-hemisphere function reflected in the WISC subtest (Similarities) that most directly measures functions subserved by the temporal area, and right-hemisphere impairment is reflected in the subtests that measure right parietal and anterior temporal functioning (Block Design and Picture Arrangement, respectively). In traumatic head injuries where one side of the cerebral cortex manifests considerable evidence of damage, it is not uncommon to find areas of the opposite side of the brain also reflecting evidence of damage resulting from the *contre coup* impact of that area of the brain against the cranial vault. The comparatively intact motor performance on the Finger Tapping Test indicates no significant involvement with the more frontal portions of either hemisphere, while the symmetrically depressed performance on the Finger Tip Number Writing Test suggests some bilateral parietal lobe dysfunction. The configuration of the more intact functions (e.g., Information, PPVT scores) reflects retention of acquired knowledge, while the configuration of the more impaired functions (e.g., Digit Span, Raven Test) includes those abilities that tend to require more synthesis of new types of information.

Although parental overprotection following his accident may play a part in the boy's poor school performance, neuropsychological evaluation clearly indicates that he has apparently suffered from a significant loss of intellectual function. The boy should be expected to profit more from special educational programming to enable him to adjust to his depressed mental capacity than from working on his motivation with psychotherapy.

Outcome Subsequent re-evaluation 1 year after the accident indicates very little improvement in his level of functioning, and suggests that substantial future improvement

Table 5. Summary of test data—Case III

Wechsler Intelligence Scale for Children
Verbal IQ 81, Performance IQ 75, Full Scale IQ 76

	Scaled score		Scaled score
Information	10	Picture Completion	8
Comprehension	9	Picture Arrangement	5
Arithmetic	6	Block Design	5
Similarities	4	Object Assembly	7
Vocabulary	8	Coding	7
Digit Span	5		

Note: On the Wechsler subscales, the mean is 10 and the standard deviation is 3.

	Standard score
Bender Visual Motor Gestalt Test	74
Draw-A-Person	85
Peabody Picture Vocabulary Test	95
Raven Progressive Matrices	74

Wide Range Achievement Test	Grade equivalent	Standard score
Reading	2.6	90
Spelling	1.7	79
Arithmetic	2.1	84

Sensory: Finger Tip Number Writing (errors per 20 presentations)
    Right 6, Left 5
Motor: Finger Oscillation (taps per 10-second period)
    Right 31.43, Left 28.10

should not be anticipated. The major forms of efforts on behalf of this youngster included counseling both his parents and teachers to scale down their expectations of his ability to perform in school. Although the parents were initially very resistive to accepting the fact that their son's intellectual limitations might be expected to preclude college work or even average-level elementary and secondary school work, after several counseling sessions covering a 6-month period the parents were able to accept the boy's best efforts, rather than pushing him to achieve at levels beyond his newly diminished ability.

Case IV

Background   The patient is a 9-year, 6-month-old son of a draftsman father and secretary mother. He has an older sister, age 11. He sat upright at 7 months, spoke his first word at 11 months, walked at 12 months, rode a tricycle at 3 years, and enjoyed playing with his age peers and older sister before beginning school. He entered kindergarten at age 5, made satisfactory progress, and was promoted to first grade. He received Bs and Cs and was promoted to second grade, where he received mostly Cs and was promoted to third grade. His third-grade teacher reports he made a good adjustment until the first report card (C average) and then developed an increasing pattern of disturbing other students, although not to a serious extent. After Christmas holidays, his school work began to deteriorate to C-minus level, with more acting out, but not to an extent requiring more scolding by the teacher. A parent conference at this time revealed increased quarreling with his sister over the past year, less playing with school friends who lived in the neighborhood, and more time spent playing with a pet hamster. The teacher is beginning to wonder if he is too socially immature to go on to fourth grade and is considering retention in third grade to let his social maturity develop. The mother is cooperative, but puzzled, because neither she nor her older child ever had any school difficulty. The father denies any problem, says most boys act this way, reports that he was a "hell raiser" himself and repeated fourth grade, but finally settled down about seventh or eighth grade, and made good grades thereafter.

Medical   The family pediatrician examined the child and found nothing he considered to be of medical significance. At the family's insistence, the boy was referred to a pediatric neurologist, who did a standard neurological evaluation and EEG, which were normal. The neurologist did mention that the child seemed a bit tense and frustrated. The neurologist also remarked that, although the child appeared to be of normal intelligence, he did not do as well as expected on some standard reading and arithmetic problems, and suggested psychometric evaluation to see if the child were possibly of low-normal intelligence. The psychometric test results are given in Table 6.

Discussion There are a number of features suggestive of specific familial dyslexia in this case. First, of course, is the fairly large discrepancy between Wechsler IQ level and Wide Range Achievement, Reading level. Generalized left cerebral hemisphere dysfunction or developmental delay are both rea-

Table 6. Summary of test data—Case IV

Wechsler Intelligence Scale for Children
Verbal IQ 97, Performance IQ 104, Full Scale IQ 101

	Scaled score		Scaled score
Information	9	Picture Completion	13
Comprehension	11	Picture Arrangement	8
Arithmetic	9	Block Design	13
Similarities	12	Object Assembly	12
Vocabulary	9	Coding	7
Digit Span	7		

Note: On the Wechsler subscales, the mean is 10 and the standard deviation is 3.

	Standard score
Bender Visual Motor Gestalt Test	112
Draw-A-Person	105
Peabody Picture Vocabulary Test	108
Raven Progressive Matrices	102

Wide Range Achievement Test	Grade equivalent	Standard score
Reading	2.5	81
Spelling	2.4	80
Arithmetic	3.8	92

Sensory: Finger Tip Number Writing (errors per 20 presentations)
    Right 1, Left 2
Motor: Finger Oscillation (taps per 10-second period)
    Right 33.8, Left 31.0

sonably well excluded by virtue of both his developmental history and his intact current functioning on general language skills (e.g., Wechsler Verbal IQ, PPVT). His Wechsler subtest scatter represents a pattern commonly found in dyslexic children, i.e., spatial abilities (Picture Completion, Block Design, Object Assembly) all intact and elevated over his own average subtest levels, conceptual abilities (e.g., Similarities, Comprehension) all comparatively intact, and sequencing abilities (Digit Span, Picture Arrangement, Coding) all fairly uniformly depressed (Bannatyne, 1968; Hartlage, 1970). The Wechsler Verbal subtests reflecting acquired knowledge are slightly low, possibly reflecting an impoverished informational input because of inadequate reading skills. Comparisons of the two cerebral hemispheres on gross intellectual measures (e.g., PPVT vs. Bender; WISC Verbal vs. Performance IQ) and on motor (tapping) and receptive sensory functions (Finger Tip Number Writing) do not support any lateralized dysfunction, and (excluding the noticeably lower WRAT scores dealing with word recognition and spelling) all global intellectual measures are within a fairly small range. The fact that the boy's academic status went from satisfactory in kindergarten and first grade to a fairly steady decline at the present time, may reflect the increasingly greater emphasis placed on reading in middle primary grades. The additional fact that his father reports having experienced similar reading problems lends further support to a diagnosis of specific familial dyslexia (Michael-Smith, Morganstern, and Karp, 1970). In this case, the additional information provided by the two neuropsychological techniques helped to confirm the specific reading components of the disorder by providing data reflecting essentially bilateral symmetry of generalized motor and sensory functions. The emotional aspects of the problem appear to be secondary to the specific reading deficit because their onset and increase in severity coincide with his increasing academic frustrations.

There is reasonable certainty from the diagnostic battery that the child's learning problem is a fairly restricted deficit in symbolic language, and additional confirmatory data would be helpful, especially documentation of the integrity of auditory comprehension. Part of the Durrell Analysis of Reading Difficulty was subsequently given, with the following results:

Oral Reading	Grade 2.3
Silent Reading	Grade 1.9
Listening Comprehension	Grade 4.0

The Durrell results confirm that the deficit is confined to visual word recognition, and indicate intact receptive and associative auditory language skills. Switching from a reading-based curriculum to an auditory instructional approach was recommended.

Outcome Follow-up of this boy's academic progress indicates that, within a few months after an aural comprehension instructional approach was initiated to minimize the impact of his specific reading problems, his social behavior returned to its previous level. His academic achievement, although still deficient in formal reading skills, was sufficient to permit him to continue in his current grade placement. One year after the aural comprehension instructional approach had been implemented, he was functioning at approximately current grade level in all subjects except word recognition and spelling, and he was no longer considered to be in academic difficulty, although he still required the modified instructional approach. This type of (genetic) disorder represents a good example of brain dysfunction in the absence of identifiable damage.

CONCLUSIONS

The performance of specific intellectual tasks and the acquisition of specific academic skills is dependent on the integrity of that part of the brain which subserves these processes. Thus, the role of the brain in learning is not one that can be adequately described in terms of either "damaged" or "normal." There is considerable specialization of brain function associated with given sides or loci, and a meaningful approach to understanding the involvement of the brain in a learning disability can be enhanced by attempting to evaluate the functional integrity of specific brain areas that subserve performance on specific intellective or learning tasks.

Although there are no direct means for determining the integrity of given areas of brain tissue or the functional interactions between different brain areas, it is possible, using psychometric, motor, and sensory assessment procedures, to measure given skills subserved by specific brain areas and to use these data to help evaluate the status of the underlying brain tissue. For such purposes, some basic knowledge of brain topography and the involvement of given brain areas in specific functions can provide the school psychologist with a more sophisticated approach toward the diagnosis of and factors involved in a specific learning disability. This knowledge will enable him to interpret psychometric data in terms of the information relative to brain status that they can provide.

A number of commonly used psychometric tests and two easily administered measures of motor and sensory hemispheric asymmetry from the Reitan neuropsychological battery have been used to illustrate how the school psychologist can begin to measure the function of each cerebral hemisphere, identify anterior or posterior extent and severity of dysfunctions, and whether they are chronic or acute.

In terms of treatment or remedial implications, the use of a neuropsychological interpretive approach can identify the unimpaired brain systems that can be used as optimal channels for remedial or compensatory educational programming. Such an approach can also identify those brain systems whose impairment precludes the likelihood of gain from remedial programs dependent upon the functional integrity of these specific brain areas.

LITERATURE CITED

Bannatyne, A. D. 1968. Diagnosing learning disabilities and writing remedial prescriptions. J. Learn. Disab. 1(4).

Brain, R. 1961. Speech Disorders: Aphasia, Apraxia and Agnosia. Butterworth, London.

Critchley, M. 1953. The Parietal Lobes. Arnold, London.

Fitzhugh, K. B., Fitzhugh, L. C., and Reitan, R. M. 1961. Psychological deficits in relation to acuteness of brain dysfunction. J. Consult. Psych. 25:61–66.

Fitzhugh, K. B., Fitzhugh, L. C., and Reitan, R. M. 1962. Wechsler-Bellevue comparisons in groups with "chronic" and "current" lateralized and diffuse brain lesions. J. Consult. Psych. 26:306–310.

Fitzhugh, K. B., Fitzhugh, L. C., and Reitan, R. M. 1963. Effects of "chronic" and "current" lateralized and non-lateralized cerebral lesions upon trial making test performances. J. Nerv. Ment. Dis. 137:82–87.

Halstead, W. C. 1947. Brain and Intelligence. University of Chicago Press, Chicago.

Hartlage, L. C. 1970. Differential diagnosis of dyslexia, minimal brain damage and emotional disturbances in children. Psychology in the Schools 7(4):403–406.

Hartlage, L. C., and Green, J. B. 1971. EEG differences in children's reading, spelling and arithmetic abilities. Percept. Mot. Skills 32:133–134.

Hartlage, L. C., and Green, J. B. 1972. EEG abnormalities and WISC subtest differences. J. Clin. Psych. 28(2):180–171.

Hartlage, L. C., and Green, J. B. 1973. The EEG as a predictor of intellective and academic performance. J. Learn. Disab. 6(4): 42–45.

Hartlage, L. C., and Lucas, D. G. 1972. Predicting reading ability in first grade children. Percept. Mot. Skills 34:231–232.

Hartlage, L. C., and Lucas, D. G. 1973a. Mental Development: Evaluation of the Pediatric Patient. Charles C Thomas, Springfield, Ill.

Hartlage, L. C., and Lucas, D. G. 1973b. Group screening for reading disability in first grade children. J. Learn. Disab. 6(5):48–52.

Hartlage, L. C., Lucas, D. G., and Main, W. H. 1972. Comparisons of three approaches to teaching reading skills. Percept. Mot. Skills 34:231–232.

Hartlage, P. L., and Hartlage, L. C. 1973. Comparisons of hyperlexic and dyslexic children. Neurology 23(4):436–437.

Keogh, B. 1969. The Bender-Gestalt with children: Research implications. J. Spec. Educ. 3:19–22.

Klatskin, E. H., McNamara, N. E., Shaffer, D., and Pincus, J. H. 1972. Minimal organicity in children of normal intelligence: Correspondence between psychological test results and neurological findings. J. Learn. Disab. 5(4):37–42.

Kløve, H. 1959. Relationship of differential electroencephalographic patterns to distribution of Wechsler-Bellevue scores. Neurology 9: 871–876.

Koppitz, E. M. 1970. Brain damage, reading disability, and the Bender-Gestalt Test. J. Learn. Disab. 3:429–433.

Lacks, P. B., Colbert, J., Harrow, M., and Leveine, J. 1970. Further evidence concerning the diagnostic accuracy of the Halstead Organic Test battery. J. Clin. Psych. 480–481.

Luria, A. 1965. Neuropsychological analysis of focal brain lesions. In: B. Wolman (ed.), Handbook of Clinical Psychology. McGraw-Hill, New York.

Michael-Smith, H., Morganstern, M., and Karp, E. 1970. Dyslexia in four siblings. J. Learn. Disab. 3(4):185–193.

Nielsen, J. M. 1946. Agnosia, Apraxia, Aphasia: Their Value in Cerebral Localization. Hoenber, New York.

Reed, H. B. C., Reitan, R. M., and Kløve, H. 1965. The influence of cerebral lesions on psychological test performances of older children. J. Consult. Psych. 29:247–251.

Reitan, R. M. 1955. Certain differential effects of left and right cerebral lesions in human adults. J. Compar. Physiol. Psych. 48: 474–477.

Reitan, R. M. 1964. Psychological deficits resulting from cerebral lesions in man. In: J. M. Warren and K. Akert (eds.), The Frontal Granular Cortex and Behavior. McGraw-Hill, New York.

Reitan, R. M. 1971. Trail making test results for normal and brain-damaged children. Percept. Mot. Skills 33:575–581.

Reitan, R. M., and Tarshes, E. L. 1959. Differential effects of lateralized brain lesions on the trail making test. J. Nerv. Ment. Dis. 129–262.

Shipley, W. C. 1940. A self-administered scale for measuring intellectual impairment and deterioration. J. Psych. 9:371–377.

Tarnopol, L., and Tarnopol, M. 1976. Reading and learning disabilities in the United States. In: L. Tarnopol and M. Tarnopol (eds.), Reading Disabilities: An International Perspective, pp. 312–314. University Park Press, Baltimore.

Chapter 5

Auditory Information Processing and Learning Disabilities

Edmond Henry Keir

Many slow-learning children have been referred for audiology tests who were considered by teachers, physicians, psychologists, speech therapists, and parents to have "auditory problems." These referrals were characteristically made on the basis of the children's observed inconsistent or confused responses to speech in the classroom, the clinic, or the home. The most frequent complaint was that their "auditory discrimination" was poor, and this tentative diagnosis was often based on the children's poor performance on discrimination tests such as the Wepman Test (Wepman, 1958). The audiologist was frequently asked to confirm this poor auditory discrimination by testing and to suggest appropriate remedial measures.

Working with these children, it soon became clear that their auditory problems were seldom, if at all, related either to a previously unsuspected partial deafness or to an inability

---

This chapter is generally concerned with auditory processes that are mediated by the left temporal lobe. Because the tests used do not readily lend themselves to direct interpretations of specific areas of brain function, no attempt is made to indicate such premature interpretations of the data (the editors).

to discriminate adequately among the phonemes of speech. With almost no exceptions, the children had normal audiograms. In the acoustically controlled conditions of the test room they performed well enough on both difference-limen frequency tests (pure-tone hearing tests) and on standardized phonetically balanced word-discrimination tests, ruling out the possibility that discrimination, per se, was at fault. These negative test results, however, proved to be of small comfort to the person who referred the child because they did not give any explanation for the child's erratic auditory responses that had been observed in the classroom, clinic, or home. It then became clear that if the audiologist were to contribute meaningfully to the management of these somehow auditorily disadvantaged children, a new way of looking at auditory perceptual functioning had to be found and new testing techniques devised.

THE AUDITORY PROBLEM

In the typical classroom learning situation, the child depends very heavily upon the normal functioning of his auditory modality for the successful reception, integration, and assimilation of new information and knowledge (Zigmond, 1969), and the role that audition plays in learning remains a crucial one throughout the child's school life. Despite this fact, to date there has been very little coordinated, in-depth research into problems of auditory perception.

Consequently, the classroom teacher confronted by a number of children with different auditory difficulties (one child unable to sequence auditory information, another unable to see that "c-at" synthesises into "cat," yet another seemingly unable to discriminate between speech sounds) finds himself in a quandary. He is not only unable to understand fully the nature of each child's disability but also is unable to decide which, if any, remedial procedure is appropriate to the particular problem noted.

There are three main reasons for this unsatisfactory state of affairs. First, there has been no definitive theory of auditory perception broad enough to explain the variety of auditory problems noted in the classroom. Second, there has been a traditional lack of interest within audiology as a discipline in problems that do not involve a loss of hearing. The majority of audiologists work in clinics that are medically rather than behaviorally oriented, and when they are asked to assess problems of auditory perception, too often obtaining a normal audiogram marks the end rather than the beginning of the diagnostic process. Third, because of this lack of involvement of audiologists, there have been no serious attempts to standardize audiologically those tests that are most frequently used to describe auditory functioning. Tests such as the Wepman Auditory Discrimination Test (Wepman, 1958), The Templin Test (Templin, 1957), the Seashore Measures, Rhythm subtest (Seashore, Lewis, and Saetveit, 1960), and the various sentence and digit-span memory subtests (Wechsler and the Illinois Test of Psycholinguistic Abilities) are audiologically invalid. These tests make no attempt to control such crucial variables as stimulus quality and intensity. They can be administered by a variety of testers who may differ widely in their articulation, accent, and intonation patterns.[1] When to this is added the fact that the tests are administered under a wide range of uncontrolled and often acoustically unacceptable environments, it is not surprising that reliable and valid results are impossible to obtain and that published studies have been known to draw contradictory conclusions using the same tests (Hammill and Larsen, 1973).

THEORETICAL CONSIDERATIONS

Many psychophysical variables and processes operate between the arrival of a word or sentence at the eardrum and its ulti-

---

[1] Except the Seashore Measures, which are recorded (the editors).

mate understanding by the person. If any one of these processes is impaired, the person will experience a corresponding degree of difficulty in interpreting the auditory information he has received. Appropriate remedial work with a person thus handicapped depends upon the successful isolation of the particular process or auditory subskill that is impaired. In the absence of a workable theoretical model of auditory perception, this has been impossible to do with any precision.

Researchers attempting to understand the variables involved in the processing of visual information were faced with the similar lack of theoretical model of visual perception until one was finally supplied by information processing theorists (Haber, 1969; Lindsay and Norman, 1972). Their major contribution was the description of the dynamic processes involved in the reception, processing, and storage of visual information. The theory describes the existence of three separate visual memory subsystems—short-term sensory storage, short-term memory, and long-term memory,—and describes the flow of visual information between these systems. Information processing theory is equally applicable to the auditory modality, and, indeed, if auditory processing is studied within the framework of this theory, it finally becomes possible to define with some precision those auditory subskills upon which meaningful listening depends.

Figure 1 is a flow chart depicting events as they occur sequentially from the time the auditory signal (speech mixed with environmental noise) arrives at the eardrum until the signal is finally understood and incorporated into one's permanent store of knowledge. Using a visual analogy, the flow chart can be conceptualized as an operating system comprising three separate storage systems (short-term auditory storage, short-term auditory memory, and long-term memory) between each of which are sorting and recording processes.

The function of the receptive mechanism (middle ear and cochlea) is to transform the sound waves arriving at the drum into electrical activity, which it does accurately unless pre-

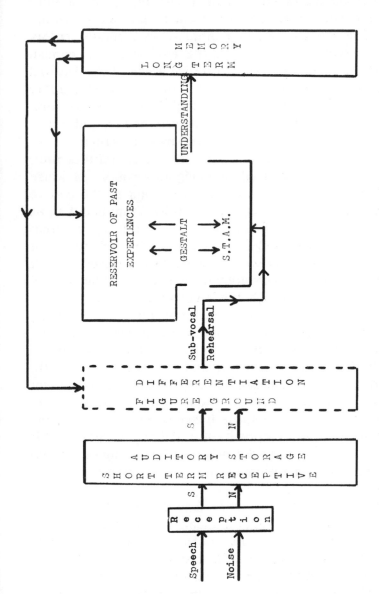

Figure 1. The auditory perceptual process. The schematic diagram depicts the flow of auditory information. Three central nervous system (CNS) storage facilities are postulated: short-term memory storage, lasting about 1.5 seconds; short-term auditory memory (STAM), following subvocal rehearsal; and long-term memory. Sorting and recoding processes include figure-ground differentiation, rehearsal, auditory gestalt, and understanding by comparing the signal with past experiences.

vented by some malfunction. Thus transformed, the auditory information (both speech and noise) enters short-term auditory storage. This storage system maintains an accurate sensory image of everything that arrives at the sense organ long enough to permit the higher processes to decide which of the received information is relevant. The presence of short-term auditory storage has been demonstrated by Inglis (1965). Information can be held in short-term storage only very briefly, and a time of 1 to 1.5 seconds has been mentioned by some writers.

This period of time is sufficient for the central processes, which continually monitor all incoming information, to decide which of the auditory information is relevant to the task at hand and is to be accepted and which is irrelevant and is to be rejected. This sorting of the relevant information (speech) from the irrelevant (noise) is accomplished by the process of *figure-ground differentiation,* which can be described as a sort of receptive filter programmed by the mental set of the listener.

Having passed through this figure-ground filter, the selected information (speech) is then transformed into short-term memory by a process involving subvocal (silent) rehearsal. Subvocal rehearsal is essential for information to be transformed into short-term memory, and if it is interfered with, the information held in sensory storage disappears and cannot be recalled (Warrington, 1971). The information in short-term memory is no longer a complete image of what arrived at the sense organ but is an interpretation of the relevant part of this material. Coding at this level "reflects the meaning of the material being thought about and not its actual physical content" (Lindsay and Norman, 1972).

Short-term auditory memory may be looked upon as a temporary holding reservoir for incoming coded auditory information. It has a limited capacity for the number of discrete units of information that it can hold at any one time. The role it plays in the successful processing of auditory information is a crucial one. Auditory data are both transient and sequential in nature, and the all-important task of short-term memory is to accumulate and hold arriving units of auditory information (phonemes, words, phrases) long enough for them to build up into a pattern that can be recognized by the listener.

As the auditory information arrives and accumulates in short-term auditory memory, it is continually being thought about and compared with the information available to the person from his reservoir of past experiences (Figure 1). Understanding finally comes when this constant scanning suddenly produces a remembered experience that matches the information accumulating in short-term memory. This recognition of meaning, this sudden equating of the gradually built-up and sometimes incomplete auditory pattern with a past experience, is the process of auditory gestalt, or closure. Auditory gestalt is the last process in the auditory perceptual chain, and it must function successfully for the final recoding of information to take place. This final recoding involves the transfer of information from short-term memory into long-term memory and allows the short-term memory system to begin processing the next batch of data.

DIAGNOSIS AND REMEDIATION

The isolation of the several subskills upon which successful auditory perceptual functioning depends has made possible the development of an audiological battery of perceptual tests to measure the relative development of these skills in the individual child. This battery of tests, when applied to the child who is somehow auditorily disadvantaged in the classroom, makes it possible to assess that child's relative perceptual strengths and weaknesses and finally to devise and perscribe a remedial auditory program tailored to his specific needs. The audiological test battery now routinely being administered to children referred for investigation of suspected auditory problems consists of a test of hearing acuity (pure tone audiogram), a test

of speech discrimination, and four tests of perceptual functioning. These include: Test of Short-Term Auditory Storage,
Figure-Ground Differentiation Test, Short-Term Auditory
Memory Test, and Test of Auditory Gestalt. Some preliminary
findings from the administration of these tests to children with
learning problems are presented here. Because the battery of
perceptual tests has been developed over a period of some
years, some tests will have been in use for a considerable time,
while others have been developed recently. Thus, the size of
the sample of children tested will vary with each test.

The sample, "learning-problem children," is defined as
those children who have presented to the clinic with at least
a 2-year delay in reading age, or some younger children who,
despite 12 months at school, have not been able to master any
elementary reading skills. In each case, other assessments will
have revealed at least some areas of age-appropriate functioning in each child.

PURE-TONE AUDIOMETRY

Every perceptual modality depends upon the intactness of its
receptive mechanism for optimum functioning because this
mechanism controls both the strength and the quality of the incoming signal. In the auditory system, defects of reception
can arise either as the result of a fault in mechanical reception
(middle ear or conductive deafness) or as a lesion in the en-
coding apparatus (cochlea or sensorineural deafness). Conductive deafness reduces the strength of the incoming signal,
while sensorineural deafness distorts the signal as well. Thus,
every investigation of the hearing modality must include a
measure of the intactness of the receptive mechanism, and
therefore a pure-tone audiogram is the essential first step in
assessment.

Pure-tone audiometry has been carried out in every one
of the total sample of 240 children with learning problems.
Only one child was found to have previously undiagnosed

sensorineural deafness severe enough to contribute significantly to his learning difficulties. He had severe high-tone sensorineural loss for frequencies over 1,000 Hz (cps) and could not discriminate among any of the higher frequency speech sounds (s, t, k, f, ch, p, sh, th, h). Thirty-eight children had mild conductive hearing losses resulting from upper respiratory tract infections, and they were referred for appropriate otological treatment. These findings are summarized in Table 1.

The absence of a greater number of children with undiagnosed sensorineural hearing losses in the sample is a reflection of the efficacy of the school entry audiometric screening service provided by the local school medical service. The large number of cases with mild fluctuating conductive deafness in the sample is not unusual. Many writers have commented on the high incidence of such hearing losses in children in their first 2 or 3 years at school. This high incidence should emphasize the fact that is should be the duty of every teacher (certainly of every remedial teacher) to ensure that none of the children in his class is unnecessarily handicapped by even a mild hearing impairment. Quick and effective hearing screening tests are readily available. The Royal National Institute for the Deaf (RNID) hearing screening test is particularly effective (Reed, 1960) and is also useful as a test of speech discrimination.

AUDITORY DISCRIMINATION

One hundred and twelve of the total sample of 240 children with hearing problems presented with suspected reduced ability to discriminate among the sounds of speech. The suspicion that auditory discrimination was defective arose either from observation of the child's responses in the classroom and clinic or on the basis of "discrimination" tests such as the Wepman Test (Wepman, 1958) or the Templin Test (Templin, 1957). Standardized phonetically balanced speech-discrimination tests that have been an integral part of audiological testing for many years were administered to each child.

Table 1. Pure-tone hearing tests: 240 learning-
problem children

Normal hearing	201
Mild conductive loss	38
Sensorineural loss	1

Testing

Audiological speech-discrimination tests are based on prerecorded, monosyllabic word lists that are phonetically balanced
to approximate the phonemic content of spoken English (Davis
and Silverman, 1969; Hirsch, 1952). These prerecorded tests
are presented to the subject via audiometer headphones at
exactly 40 dB[2] above his measured speech reception (hearing)
threshold, at which level maximum discrimination ability is
assured. The subject has to repeat words that are presented by
a carrier phrase (e.g., "Please say, 'thing'") at 5-second intervals. The number of errors made on each list is noted, and a
percentage discrimination score is derived (Katz, 1972). If the
child's defective articulation prevents his response from being
readily recognized by the tester, a modified prerecorded test
is used. In this test the child is asked (again via headphones)
to point to one of a series of pictures that are grouped so that
they provide a measure of both vowel and consonant discrimination (e.g., cot, cat, kite; cap, tap, hat). Again, a percentage
discrimination score is derived, and in each case a score of 90
percent or better is taken to indicate that the child's ability
to discriminate between speech sounds is functionally adequate,
that is, he would not be handicapped in any social listening
situation.

Results

The results of speech-discrimination testing are found in Table
2. A total of 229 children had no trouble passing the audiolo-

---

[2] About the loudness of ordinary speech for a normal person (the editors).

Table 2. Audiological speech discrimination tests: 240 learning-problem children

Discrimination score (%)	Number of cases
91–100 (Normal)	229
81–90 (Mildly abnormal)	8
Below 81 (Abnormal)	3

gically standardized test of speech discrimination at the 90-percent level and must be regarded as having normal speech-discrimination ability. Only 11 children failed at the 90-percent level. Of these, eight failed only minimally (scores between 80 and 90 percent) and cannot be regarded as having discrimination problems serious enough to warrant extensive remediation. Of the three children who scored less than 80 percent, one was the boy with the high-tone sensorineural loss described earlier (score, 52 percent). The remaining two children (scores of 65 and 70 percent were the only others found to have speech-discrimination problems severe enough to affect their learning performance significantly.

Table 3 summarizes the outcome of speech-discrimination testing in the 112 cases of children who were referred for discrimination problems. Of the 71 children thought by teachers

Table 3. Audiological speech discrimination tests: 112 learning-problem children with suspected speech discrimination difficulties

Discrimination score (%)	Number of cases		
	Suspected by teachers or clinicians	Poor Wepman Test scores	Totals
91–100 (Normal)	64	38	102
81–90 (Mildly abnormal)	6	2	8
Below 81 (Abnormal)	1	1	2
Totals	71	41	112

or clinicians to have significant discrimination problems, only one child did have such problems. Of the 41 children thought to have speech-discrimination problems on the basis of their poor scores on the Wepman Test, again only one child did have such problems.

Comments

These results seem to question seriously whether tests such as the Wepman really measure speech-discrimination ability per se, or whether poor scores on such tests merely reflect differences resulting from the effects of variables other than discrimination, which may be inherent either in the test itself or in its administration. The present study suggests that the latter explanation is the correct one. All tests that purport to measure discrimination by asking the child to make a judgment about the sameness or difference of two consecutively presented phonemes or words can be criticized on several grounds. First, the tests presuppose that the child has the language sophistication necessary to follow the quite complicated test requirements. Second, the tests all suffer from lack of audiological standardization. This makes it very difficult to compare results obtained on separate occasions because no two testers possess speech patterns identical in pitch, accent, and intonation, nor are any two tests carried out under completely identical acoustic conditions. Third, the use of these tests is difficult to justify with children who have articulation defects (Keir, 1973).

The inescapable conclusion is that it is difficult to justify the time spent in remedial activities aimed at giving the child extensive practice in the discrimination of speech sounds if the sole reason for doing so is the child's poor scores on an audiologically unstandardized "discrimination" test.

SHORT-TERM AUDITORY STORAGE

Short-term auditory storage is the system that holds all incoming auditory data (speech and noise) long enough for the central processes to decide which to attend to and which to disregard. Short-term auditory storage capacity is most readily measured with a test of dichotic listening, which arose out of the experiments of Broadbent (1956) who was originally investigating cerebral dominance in listening. In this test, two different series of digits are presented simultaneously, one to each ear, and the subject is asked to recall both series. The test depends on the fact that the human mind can only attend to one item of information at a time, so that when two series are presented simultaneously, one of them is attended to immediately and the second is held in short-term auditory storage until the mind is ready to attend to it. Inglis (1965), in an ingenious series of experiments, showed that when two simultaneously presented series were recalled, errors in recall occurred in the series that was held in short-term storage.

Testing

In the present study, a two-track tape recorder was used to record two separate series of digits simultaneously, one on each track, at the rate of one digit every half second, for example,

Track one	1	4	9
Track two	2	6	5

The different series increased in length from one digit in each to a maximum of five in each. The series were presented binaurally (to both ears simultaneously) via audiometer headphones at 40 dB above the speech reception threshold in each ear, and the child was asked to repeat as many numbers as he could.

Results

The results of the dichotic listening test are shown in Table 4. The present author has only recently begun to use this test, and so only a small number of children have been tested. Of the 20 children aged 8 years shown in Table 4, the control group of 10 could recall an average of 5.8 numbers, while the

Table 4. Dichotic listening tests: 8-year-old children

Number of digits recalled	Control group (N = 10)	Learning problem group (N = 10)	t	p
Mean	5.8	4.2	9.4	0.001
Standard deviation	1.33	1.05		

t, test for the significance of the difference between means.
p, probability level of the t-test score.

mean score of those in the learning problem group was 4.2. The number of cases tested so far is, of course, far too small to allow any generalizations to be made. Further testing to produce developmental norms for short-term auditory storage capacity is continuing.[3]

Comments

The practical implications of severe defects of short-term auditory storage to the learning process are interesting, particularly with respect to reading. Typically, learning to read involves the simultaneous presentation of the written symbol (phoneme or word) and its auditory equivalent. Caird (1961) replicated this situation by the simultaneous presentation of a series of digits one-at-a-time visually and a different series auditorily. He found that the same rules for recall applied to this situation as for dichotic listening. The visually dominant subjects (80 percent of the population are visually dominant) attended to the visual series first, and the remaining 20 percent (auditorily dominant) attended to the auditory series first. Once again, if mistakes were made, they were made in the series (visual or auditory) that had to be held in short-term receptive storage.

The implications for learning to read are clear. With 80 percent of the children (the visually dominant) the auditory stimu-

---

[3] Witelson (1962) studied a small sample of children with learning problems using a dichotic listening test. She found that these children need more time than do normal children to organize and restructure the auditory input (the editors).

lus accompanying the word or phoneme has to be held momentarily in short-term auditory storage while the mind processes the visual stimulus. If short-term auditory storage is severely defective, the recall of the auditory stimulus will suffer and opportunities for making the meaningful audio-visual associations that form the basis of reading (and virtually every learning situation) will be greatly reduced. *Thus, for those children whose short-term auditory storage is defective, simultaneous presentation of stimuli (the multisensory approach) should be avoided and care taken to present stimuli of different modalities sequentially, one at a time.*

FIGURE-GROUND DIFFERENTIATION

The role that figure-ground differentiation plays in auditory processing is that of a receptive selection filter. Programmed by the mental set of the listener, it allows the child to select that auditory information relevant to the task at hand and to reject irrelevant data. Thus, in a noisy classroom, the auditory "figure" is the teacher's voice and the "ground" is the background or environmental noise. Children with poor figure-ground differentiation skills find difficulty in isolating and attending consistently to this "figure" (teacher's voice) to the exclusion of the other transient environmental sounds ("ground").

Testing

In the test of figure-ground differentiation, the same prerecorded, phonetically balanced word lists are used as were used to measure speech-discrimination ability. The word list is presented binaurally to the child at 40 dB above his measured speech reception threshold, and a background noise of gradually increasing intensity is superimposed upon the speech. This background noise is "white" noise available on most audiometers as a masking signal and has a spectrum containing in equal proportion all of the audible (sound) frequencies. The white noise is originally introduced at a level of 15 dB below that of the speech and is gradually increased in intensity by 5-dB steps until the child can repeat only 50 percent of 10 consecutively presented words. This 50-percent discrimination point is the recognized threshold of intelligibility on audiologically standardized word-discrimination tests, and it marks the point at which the subject is just able to recognize the signal received as intelligible speech (Katz, 1972). The level of noise at which this 50-percent discrimination score is reached is noted.

Results

Standardization trials have now involved some 260 normal children from 5 to 16 years of age. In an overwhelming majority of cases (in excess of 80 percent of the sample), the 50-percent speech-discrimination score is reached when the level of the white noise is equal in intensity to the level of the presented words (Table 5). This score is taken to be a measure of normal figure-ground differentiation ability. Moreover, this score does not vary with the age of the child once the child is old enough to understand the test requirements (5 years).

One hundred and ninety-seven children with learning problems have been given this test. It is seen that 38 percent (75 of 197) of the children with learning problems had below normal scores on this test (Table 5), compared to only 15 percent (39 of 260) for the control group. Nineteen children in the sample had very severe figure-ground differentiation problems and reached the 50-percent discrimination point when the noise level was as much as 10 or (in two cases) even 15 dB below that of speech.

The results for 112 slow-learning children who originally presented with suspected speech-discrimination problems are shown in Table 6. It is seen that 59 children (more than half of this group) had problems in speech discrimination in the presence of noise. However, previous results (Table 3) showed that only two of these children had speech-discrimination problems

Table 5. Figure-ground differentiation test

	Abnormal			Normal
Background noise	− 15 dB	− 10 dB	− 5 dB	equal
Control group N = 260	0	5	34	221
		2%	13%	85%
Learning problem group	2	17	56	122
N = 197	1%	9%	28%	62%

The background noise is either 5, 10, or 15 dB below the level of the recorded speech for those children who have abnormal figure-ground discrimination ability. When the background noise and recorded speech are equal in intensity, those who pass the test are considered to have normal discrimination ability.

when tested in acoustically silent conditions. Thus, it becomes clear that it was these children's poor figure-ground differentiation skills and not discrimination problems per se which accounted for their reported confused responses to speech in the classroom.

Comments

The nature of the auditory problems that children with poor figure-ground differentiation skills have in a noisy classroom is reflected in some typical comments one hears from their teachers: "He hears me only when he wants to." "He can't pay attention." "He can hear well enough, but he won't lis-

Table 6. Figure-ground differentiation test: 112 learning-problem children with suspected discrimination problems

	Abnormal			Normal
Background noise[a]	− 15 dB	− 10 dB	− 5 dB	Equal
Number of cases	2	19	38	53
	2%	17%	34%	47%
Totals		53%		47%

[a] Noise level relative to recorded speech.

ten." Some "easily distractible" children may well have their low threshold of distractibility because of poor figure-ground differentiation. For them there is no firm distinction between the teacher's voice (the figure) to which they are supposed to be listening and the background noise. The result is confusion for the children.

Remedial procedures for children who have figure-ground differentiation problems fall into two categories. The first measures are aimed at manipulating the school environment in such a way as to highlight or intensify the stimulus figure (i.e., teacher's voice) at the expense of background, classroom, noise. The child should be placed as close to the teacher as possible so that he can receive visual and lip-reading cues to supplement his auditory input. If possible, key words or phrases should be written on the chalkboard and every effort made to reduce class noise during those lessons in which critical listening is important. These children should not be considered for "open" classrooms, and the need for adequate acoustic treatment of remedial rooms cannot be stressed enough.

The second series of measures is aimed at giving the child practice and confidence in listening in the presence of noise. Pleasant, soft music can be used as the first background stimulus and can then be gradually increased in both complexity and intensity as the child gains experience. Practice can be given to the child to consciously direct his attention from ground to figure. A useful exercise is one in which a man's voice and a woman's voice are heard simultaneously on a tape recorder, each saying different sentences. The child is asked to repeat first what the woman said, then what the man said. Nonverbal figure-ground differentiation activities can be devised using a tape recorder or recorded music, for example, to get a child to recognize individual musical instruments in an orchestrated passage (e.g., the bassoon or "grandfather" in Prokofiev's *Peter and the Wolf*).

SHORT-TERM AUDITORY MEMORY

In the processing of auditory data, the role of short-term auditory memory is to accumulate and hold sequentially arriving units of auditory information long enough for them to build into a pattern that is recognizable by the listener. Children with severe short-term memory problems are educationally acutely handicapped, and it is the experience of researchers such as Zigmond (1969) that tests of short-term auditory memory differentiate between readers and nonreaders with good consistency. Problems in short-term memory affect every level of school experience and are sometimes not recognized. For example, a child with a short-term auditory memory span that enables him to hold only two discrete items of information at a time cannot possibly synthesize "hol-i-day" and may be wrongly accused of having poor synthesizing skills. Similarly, a child whose short-term memory span can only hold a sentence of no more than nine words can be accused of disobedience if he fails to follow a 12-word instruction given to him by his teacher.

Short-term Auditory Memory Testing

The major criticism of all existing and commonly used tests of short-term auditory memory is again that they make no attempt to control crucial auditory variables. For example, a child with severe figure-ground problems may score poorly on a test of short-term auditory memory if it is given in a noisy classroom. Also, the commonly used digit span tests (Wechsler, etc.) make no attempt to control visual variables, and thus it becomes possible for even a severely deaf child to have a good short-term "auditory" memory score if he has good lip-reading and visual processing skills.

The present battery of auditory memory tests attempts to overcome these problems by having all tests prerecorded by one speaker and always presented to the child under optimum acoustic conditions (binaurally via audiometer headphones at a standard 40 dB above measured speech reception thresholds). There are three subtests in the battery; these include tests of memory for digits, rhythms, and connected sentences. The standardization of these tests will not be fully described here. However, some general comments about each test are relevant.

Digit Span Test   In general, up to the age of 7, the normal child should reproduce one digit, or at the most two, fewer than his age in years when the digits are presented at 1-second intervals (i.e., three or four digits is normal for a 5-year-old child). Developmentally, this skill reaches a plateau at the age of 8 to 10 years, when most children can reproduce six, seven, or eight digits. On this test, a child is considered to have a significant memory problem if he can reproduce no more than three digits fewer than his age in years in the 7 years and younger group, or if he can reproduce fewer than five digits in the 7 years and older group.

Memory for Rhythms   There was an almost exact correlation (in the 5- to 8-year age range) between the number of digits a child could reproduce and rhythm length. Rhythm length was measured by the number of beats it contained. Thus, a child who could recall four digits could reproduce this rhythm, ' ″ ', but not this one ″ ″'. This correlation is most valuable diagnostically because a nonverbal memory test (rhythms) can be administered to young language-impaired or deaf children, and the results may be compared meaningfully with those on the digit span test administered to normal children.

Memory for Connected Sentences   The connected sentence test consists of 32 sentences, which increase in length one syllable at a time. Because grammatical structure can also affect the recall of connected sentences, care was taken to ensure that, as nearly as possible, the grammatical structure of the sentences also progressed in order of difficulty. For this, the Lee and Koenigsknecht Developmental Sentence Scoring scale was used (Lee and Koenigsknecht, 1972).

Test results indicated that *the number of words a sentence contained, rather than the number of syllables, governed whether it would be recalled or not.* It was found, in general, that children could repeat sentences containing up to two-and-a-half to three times as many words as the number of digits they could recall in the digit span test; i.e., a child with a digit span of four could recall 10- to 12-word sentences accurately.

Failure on this test was indicated if a child under the age of 8 could not repeat accurately a sentence containing fewer than the number of words equal to twice his age in years. In the 8 years and older group, a child failed if he could not repeat a sentence of 16 words or less.

Results

The short-term auditory memory test has been given to 75 slow-learning children and 75 controls. Table 7 lists the number of children in each group who failed on the various tests. It shows that 63 percent of the learning-problem children had significant difficulty with short-term auditory memory compared to 12 percent of the control group.

Comments

The very high proportion (63 percent) of children who failed the auditory memory test probably reflects a bias in the sample of children tested. The results on all of the different subtests probably give a somewhat exaggerated picture of the incidence of auditory perceptual problems in the general population of children with learning problems because children who come to an audiology unit for testing are selected on the basis of possible auditory disability. Nevertheless, some of the children reported here had very severe memory deficits. One 14-year-old boy could only recall three digits and ten-word sentences and was almost a total nonreader. Another eight-year-old girl had a digit span of two and was also perceptually not ready to learn to read.

Table 7. Short-term auditory memory tests

| | Number who failed | | | |
| | | | | |
Test	Digit span	Rhythms	Connected sentences	Average failure rate (%)
Control group $N = 75$	10	8	9	12
Learning problem group $N = 75$	48	46	46	63

The striking feature in all of the short-term memory tests is the extremely sharp and well defined cut-off point between success and failure. A child whose maximum digit span is three will reproduce three digits quickly and confidently, but when an extra digit (the fourth) is added there is often a complete breakdown in recall, with sometimes none of the presented digits reproduced. The same is true of the sentence test, in which if the short-term memory bank is overloaded, the sentence reproduced by the child may have little in common with the original. In some cases, the reproduced sentence may contain many reversals of words, and whole meaning reversals are also common. One child who could reproduce only six-word sentences accurately, produced, "The mouse chased the cat" when he was given, "The cat chased the mouse under the house." Thus, if the teacher is not aware of short-term auditory memory problems in a child and continues to give instructions in long, involved sentences, in some cases the message the child is getting can be the opposite of what was intended by the teacher.

The problems that children with severe short-term auditory memory difficulties have in everyday life are summed up by some of their comments. One 8-year-old boy with a digit span of three said, "Mum tells me to do lots of things at once. I get mixed up. I do the wrong things. I get smacked." A 14-

year-old boy who can only recall nine-word sentences said of his social studies lesson, "The teacher starts to talk and after a while, although I keep hearing his words, they don't mean anything any more." An extremely intelligent adult with a digit span of four complained of her university lectures, "I can't write down the lecturer's words directly. I have to think about them first and then I write down my own translation. I miss a lot."

Unfortunately, problems of short-term auditory memory are most intractable to remediation. Exercises in remembering and recall produce little else but acute frustration on the part of the child. Several children have now been followed over a period of 6 to 8 years, and they have all shown uniformly slow maturation in short-term memory, regardless of whether remedial attempts were made or not (Table 8). Only two avenues are open to the teacher. The first is to help the child live with his problem by tailoring all instructions down to the size of that child's memory span for sentences, keeping the grammatical construction simple and being prepared to repeat directions as often as is necessary for the child to grasp them. *There is no excuse for the teacher not knowing the maximum memory span of each child in her class.*

A second approach is available with older children. These children can be taught to examine longer sentences and shown how to break them into shorter semantic or conceptual units. For example, "The old man walked slowly across the road yesterday" can be recalled in two ways. One is by remembering every word, which requires a short-term memory span of nine units of information. The second way is to split the sentence into four semantic units, or "thought pictures," 1) The

Table 8. Short-term memory span for digits: one case followed for 8 years

Age (years)	6	7	8	9	10	11	12	13	14
Memory span (digits)	2	2	3	3	3	3	4	4	4

old man, 2) walked slowly, 3) across the road, 4) yesterday. The auditory recall task then becomes the much easier one of recalling four concepts rather than nine separate units of information. Thus, the child with a poor short-term auditory memory span who is taught how to group semantically can reproduce the meaning (if not the exact words) of sentences that would otherwise be beyond his scope. The university student quoted above obviously had learned to compensate for her problem in this way.

Results on the short-term auditory memory test seem to suggest that *a memory span of at least three digits is a minimum prerequisite for reading readiness. All children with a memory span below this (including some 6- and 7-year-olds) were nonreaders and remained so regardless of which teaching or remedial method was attempted.* It is felt that if a test of short-term memory were compulsory at school entry, it would isolate and prevent many cases of potential learning failure by ensuring that these children were not exposed to reading instruction until they were perceptually ready to cope with the task.

AUDITORY GESTALT

Gestalt or closure skills are fundamental to the listener's understanding of the information that is gradually arriving and accumulating in short-term auditory memory. This understanding often occurs before all of the information relevant to the concept is present, and gestalt can be described as the ability to mentally reconstitute a whole object or concept from its imperfect sensory representation. It is this process which enables a person presented with three dots spaced as if at the corners of a triangle to say "triangle" if asked what shape the dots represent (even though all he sees are three dots). A similar auditory gestalt process enables a child to recognize "cat" if he is just given the three individual sounds "c-a-t," or to provide the last word in an uncompleted sentence such as, "Fire is hot, but ice is --" (grammatical gestalt).

Children with gestalt or closure problems are handicapped in two main ways in the classroom. First, in a busy classroom there are so many distractions that the child is very rarely able to receive an uninterrupted auditory message from the teacher and has to rely on his grammatical closure skills to fill in the missing gaps. Grammatical closure skills can be assessed by such tests as the Illinois Test of Psycholinguistic Abilities. The second way relates to the closure skills upon which all phonic synthesis depends; i.e., "b-ed" cannot be perceived as "bed" unless the child can make the necessary gestalt from the original imperfect auditory pattern ("b-ed") with which he has been presented. So far no audiologically acceptable tests of this closure skill have been devised.

Closure Test

The present test of auditory gestalt (closure) is based loosely upon interrupted voice tests that have been devised originally (Miller and Licklider, 1950) as measures of central hearing impairment. The test stimulus is a prerecorded, spondaic, (two-syllable) word list consisting of words familiar to children. Each word is preceded by a carrier phrase, i.e., "Please say -- schoolboy." The words are again presented binaurally at 40 dB above measured speech reception thresholds. Between the tape recorder and the audiometer is located an electronic interruptor switch that can be adjusted to interrupt variably the speech signal from 10 times per second to 2 times per second. Thus, the child receives fragments of the word interspersed by equal periods of silence, and, in order to respond appropriately, he has to mentally reconstitute the fragmented word.

The child is presented with six words at each of the following interruption rates: ten per second, eight per second, six per second, four per second, and two per second. In this way, progressively larger amounts of verbal information are omitted. The point is noted at which the child is unable to repeat correctly at least three of the six words presented at each level.

Results

Adults and older children (more than 7 years of age) have no difficulty in repeating all of the words correctly at interruption rates of ten, eight, and six per second. They make one or two errors at the rate of four per second and reach the 50-percent discrimination point when the words are interrupted twice a second. At present, developmental norms for this test are being obtained. Although these are as yet incomplete, it appears that children under the age of 4 are unable to cope with even the minimal interruptions inherent in the fastest switching rate (10 per second). Four-year-old children can generally repeat half of the words correctly at the ten or eight per second switching rate, while the 5-year-olds tend to reach the 50-percent point at six interruptions per second. The adult score (50 percent at two interruptions per second) is reached at about the age of 7. These preliminary findings are summarized in Table 9.

The test of auditory gestalt has now been given to 45 children of varying ages with learning problems. The point at which they reached 50-percent discrimination is summarized in Table 10. Of particular interest in this table are the three children who reached the 50-percent score at 10 interruptions per second and the seven children who reached this point at eight interruptions per second. Not one of these children (all aged 6 and 7 years) was able to cope with even the simplest exercises in phonic synthesis in the classroom. The other 35 children could all cope with phonic synthesis at some level. These results seem to indicate that, before children can cope with phonic synthesis, they must have a gestalt process developed to the point where they are able to reconstitute satisfactorily on this test words that are fragmented by being subjected to six or less interruptions per second.

Table 9. Auditory gestalt testing: minimum age which children can achieve 50-percent discrimination for various interruption rates of recorded words

Interruption rate (times per second)	10	8	6	4	2
Age (years)	4	4	5	6	7+

Comments

The test of auditory gestalt shows that some children at school entry are perceptually unready to cope with the task of phonic synthesis and that nothing but confusion and frustration can result from the teacher persisting with this task until the child is maturationally ready for it. This survey has shown that all children, given time, will eventually be able to cope with this task. The clear message to teachers faced by a child who cannot synthesize (blend) is to avoid phonically based reading approaches and, if necessary, to use one of the many available visual "look-say" schemes.

Remediation activities can include both verbal and non-verbal material. In the verbal area the child can be given practice in reconstituting connected speech in the form of simple sentences or stories, recorded first with a minimum amount of information omitted, then progressively increasing in dif-

Table 10. Auditory gestalt testing: 45 learning-disabled children 6 and 7 years old

Interruption rate (times per second)	10	8	6	4	2
Number of children scoring 50 percent or more correct responses	3	7	5	10	20

The 10 children (22 percent) who could succeed at only the eight and ten times per second interruption rates were unable to cope with even the simplest phonic syntheses. All others were able to blend words at some level.

ficulty. Phonic awareness programs such as the "T-Scheme" devised by Nugent (1972) are also useful by providing activities designed to make the child more aware of this phonetic structure of language. Nonverbal material can involve games requiring the child to recognize familiar tunes or environmental sounds that have been recorded with varying amounts of verbal information omitted.

SUMMARY

This chapter suggests a theoretical model (information processing theory) within whose framework auditory perception can be meaningfully studied. It isolates auditory perceptual subskills upon which meaningful listening depends and suggests testing techniques and remedial measures relevant to those various subskills. It suggests the need for routine school entry screening tests to isolate those children whose auditory perceptual skills are insufficiently mature to cope with the demands placed upon them by the formal learning situation.

LITERATURE CITED

Broadbent, D. 1956. Successive responses to simultaneous stimuli. Q. J. Exp. Psych. 8:145.

Caird, W. 1961. The short term storage of auditory and visual two channel digits. J. Ment. Sci. 1062.

Davis, H., and Silverman, S. R. 1969. Hearing and Deafness. Holt, Rinehart and Winston, London.

Haber, R. N. 1969. Information Processing Approaches to Visual Perception. Holt, Rinehart and Winston, New York.

Hammill, D., and Larsen, S. C. 1973. The Relationship of Selected Auditory Skills and Reading Ability. University of Texas Press, Austin.

Hirsch, I. J. 1952. Development of materials for speech audiometry. J. Speech Hear. Disord. 17:321–337.

Inglis, J. 1965. Dichotic listening and cerebral dominance. Acta Octolaryng. 60:231.

Katz, J. 1972. Handbook of Clinical Audiology. Williams & Wilkins, Baltimore,

Keir, E. H. 1973. The diagnosis and treatment of auditory perceptual deficits. In: AUSPELD Workshop Proceedings. Wymond Morell, Sydney, Australia.

Lee, L., and Koenigsknecht, R. A. 1972. Developmental Sentence Scoring. Northwestern University Press, Evanston, Ill.

Lindsay, R. H., and Norman, D. A. 1972. Human Information Processing. Academic Press, New York.

Miller, G. A., and Licklider, J. C. 1950. J. Acoust. Soc. Am. 22:167.

Nugent, C. 1972. T-Scheme. Heinemann, Melbourne.

Reed, M. 1960. RNID Hearing Test Cards. Royal National Institute for the Deaf, London.

Seashore, C. E., Lewis, D. and Saetveit, J. G. 1960. Seashore Measures of Musical Talents. Psychological Corp. New York.

Templin, M. C. 1957. Institute of Child Welfare Monograph Series, No. 26. University Press, Minneapolis.

Warrington, E. G. 1971. Neurological disorders of memory. Br. Med. Bull. 27(3):000.

Wepman, J. 1958. Auditory Discrimination Test. Language Research Associates, Chicago.

Witelson, S. 1962. Perception of auditory stimuli in children with learning problems. Unpublished masters thesis, McGill University, Montreal.

Zigmond, N. K. 1969. Auditory processes in children with learning disabilities. In: L. Tarnopol (ed.), Learning Disabilities: Introduction to Educational and Medical Management, pp. 196–216. Charles C Thomas, Springfield, Ill.

Chapter 6

Perceptual and Cortical Immaturity in Developmental Dyslexia

Dirk J. Bakker
and
Jan de Wit

Language, written and spoken, is a means of communication unique to man. In written language, by grouping a number of visual symbols in a specified way the message is set down. For the message to be understood it is necessary, among other things, that the printed symbols be correctly interpreted. This reading process is subject to certain rules, but not all the rules are the same everywhere. In English one reads from left to right, but in some languages one reads from right to left or from top to bottom. Generally the rules for reading are quite

A few sections in this chapter were taken from a contribution of the authors to a Dutch publication on child psychology: de Wit, J., and Bakker, D. J. 1971. Leesstoornissen. In: J. de Wit, H. Bolle, and R. Jessurum Cardozo-Van Hoorn (eds.), Psychologen over het Kind, deel 2, pp. 177–192. Tjeenk Willink, Groningen. The authors wish to express their gratitude to the publisher, Tjeenk Willink, BV, who kindly consented to the publication of this material, and appreciation is also extended to Miny and Nicholas Den Hartog for their English translation and comments on the maniscript.

177

complicated. Often they are based on convention and are not logically derived. Some examples may serve to illustrate this. The same letter "a" is pronounced differently in *dak* (tall) and *daken* (tale), whereas "ij" (ay) and "ei" (ey) represent the same sound, for instance in *wij* (they) and *wei* (play).

Word meanings can also be a source of difficulty. The word *slot* (board) has several meanings and yet each has a different meaning from the word *stol* (broad), even though the same letter symbols are used. Thus the meaning of a word is determined in part by the sequence of the letters. The same holds for the order of words in a sentence. "John is coming home," and "Is John coming home?" have different meanings. Besides the letters in numerous forms, one must, in reading, deal with signs such as commas, semicolons, periods, exclamation marks, question marks, and so forth. There is also the problem of type styles. The grapheme *a* looks one way in the primer, another way in a newspaper, and may appear in another style on a cereal box. Now picture the dilemma of a child of six learning to read!

Formal teaching of reading usually begins in the first grade. Many children can read fluently by the time they leave elementary school. Unfortunately, however, this is not true of all children. The efforts of some children result in only scanty rewards. These children are the ones with reading problems, and it is they who form, in part, the student body of the schools for learning and behavior disorders in the Netherlands.

The cause of the reading problem is somewhat evident. It may be related to things such as brain damage; visual, auditory or speech impairment; or low general intelligence. Finally, personality factors and social circumstances can play an important role in reading ability in general and reading disabilities in particular. Though the cause of the reading problem may sometimes be clear, this is not always the case. There are children whose reading difficulties cannot be ascribed to any of these factors. In these cases one usually speaks of *specific reading disorders.*

At the Pedological Institute of Amsterdam, these authors began investigations of the etiological determinants of specific reading disorders about 15 years ago. The emphasis has been on the relationships between perceptual factors and reading disorders as well as on the neuropsychological substrates of both.

REVIEW OF STUDIES ON READING DISORDERS

Sensory Dominance and Reading Disability

Sensory dominance has been defined as the preferred use and better performance of one sensory modality over others (Bakker, 1967b). There are indications that in the course of development changes occur in the hierarchical organization of the different sensory systems. Initially, it seems the child obtains information mainly via proximal sensation (taste, touch, proprioception), while at a later age the distal receptors (eyes, ears) take up that task. Birch (1962) suggested that this development may be abnormal in dyslexics. For example, when the dominance of the visual reception system is insufficiently developed, concurrent proprioceptive stimuli can interfere with the processing of visual information during reading. A reading disorder may result.

Three experiments in the present authors' laboratory investigated the relationship between sensory dominance and reading ability. Normal and reading-disabled children, aged 9 to 14 years, participated in the first experiment (Bakker, 1966). The dyslexics had a reading lag of at least 1 year, while the normal children were at grade level or above. The groups were matched on age, sex, and IQ. Mean age and IQ (Wechsler Intelligence Scale for Children (WISC)) for all subjects (28 boys and 4 girls) were 11.5 years and 94, respectively. The visual and proprioceptive sensitivities of the children were measured. The differences, visual sensitivity minus proprioceptive sensitivity, were then calculated.

It was hypothesized that smaller visual minus proprioceptive differences would be found in the reading-disturbed (less
visual dominance) than in the normal-reading children (more
visual dominance). The hypothesis was confirmed. Further
analysis revealed that normal readers and dyslexics did not
differ in proprioceptive sensitivity but did differ in visual
sensitivity. Normal readers were able to make finer visual dis-
criminations.

In the second experiment (Bakker, 1967b) 50 girls and 50
boys, 10 of each sex at each age from 7 through 11 years,
participated. All were elementary school children. As in the
first experiment, visual and proprioceptive sensitivity were
measured. Visual-proprioceptive sensitivity differences correlated positively with reading ability, that is, the stronger the
visual dominance the greater the reading ability. This relationship was found only in children of average intelligence (mean
WISC-IQ, 98); children with higher IQs (mean, 116) showed
no dominance-reading ability correlation.

The third experiment (Bakker, 1972a) was carried out
with the same subjects as in the second experiment plus 75
learning-disabled boys. The latter ranged in age from 9 to 13
years and had a mean reading lag of 2 years. The subjects were
presented a series of three letters in succession, one letter at a
time. These were presented haptically, visually, and auditorily.
Haptic presentation was done with letters cut into wood. The
blindfolded subjects were allowed to feel the letters one at a
time with both hands. Visual presentation involved showing
the same letters one at a time. For the auditory presentation,
the letter series were recorded on a tape and the children
listened to the tape. After each series was presented, two successive letters were presented again in the same mode. The
subject had to indicate whether these two letters had previously appeared first, second, or last. Visual minus haptic
scores and auditory minus haptic scores were used to measure
visual and auditory dominance, respectively. Only the audi-

tory dominance scores appeared to correlate positively with the reading scores of normal and disabled readers.

The dominance scores of normal and dyslexic boys were compared for the 9- to 11-year-old group. The subjects were individually matched on WISC-IQ (mean, 103). The visual and auditory dominance scores of the normal readers were higher than those of the dyslexic group. These group differences were not significant, however. One may conclude that the present authors' research partly supports Birch's (1962) hypothesis that there is a relationship between dominance of the distal (visual and auditory) receptors and reading ability. However, the hypothesis that a lack of visual and auditory dominance over the haptic sense leads to interference of concurrent haptic stimuli with visual and auditory information processing during reading remains to be proven.

**Temporal Order Perception,
Reading Disability, and Sex Differences**

Reading requires the ability to integrate spatial and temporal patterns. Printed letters and words are ordered in space from left to right, while sounds (phonemes) are ordered in time. On the basis of this analysis, experiments have been set up in which auditory-temporal and visual-spatial patterns had to be judged on equivalence. It was shown that this is much more difficult for dyslexic than for normal readers in a series of investigations carried out by Birch and Belmont (1964, 1965, 1966) and by Rudnick, Sterritt, and Flax (1967). The procedure in these investigations was generally the following: The investigator tapped a rhythmic pattern then placed before the subject a card visually depicting the pattern along with two alternatives. The subject had to point out the pattern he had just heard.

The intersensory integration measured in this way not only differentiates normal and specific reading-disabled children but also correlates with reading ability in general (Lovell and Gorton, 1968). An investigation by Blank, Weider, and Bridger (1968) indicated that defective sensory integration may be a causitive factor in specific reading disturbances, and not vice versa. In their investigation, the children participating had scarcely had any reading instruction.

In considering these experiments, it may be asked where the children's difficulties arise. Are they in the auditory-visual, in the temporal-spatial, or in both forms of integration? Blank and Bridger (1966) and Blank, Weider, and Bridger (1968) were the first to give some attention to this question. They had subjects judge the equivalence of visually presented temporal and spatial patterns. This assignment, which required only visual temporal-spatial integration, also proved more difficult for the reading-disabled than for the normal-reading children. But more was evident; merely perceiving and remembering temporal patterns was found to be a problem for reading-disabled children, at least under certain conditions. This became apparent when Blank and Bridger had their subjects reproduce tapped out temporal (rhythmic) patterns. In one assignment the pattern had to be retapped, in another the patterns had to be imitated verbally. In the verbal repetition, after the tapped out pattern ••• • had been presented, the subject would react with "one-to-three, four." It was only in this type of problem where the patterns had to be imitated verbally that difficulties arose for the dyslexic subjects. This was an important finding and led to the conclusion that *some reading-disabled children have difficulty remembering temporal patterns only when a verbal medium is used.*

Above-average Disabled Readers versus Below-average Disabled Readers   In a first study (Bakker, 1967a), meaningful figures, meaningless figures, letters, and numerals were presented in temporal succession. Presentation time for each stimulus was 2 seconds; the interval between two stimuli was 4 seconds. The subjects, students of a school for children with learning difficulties and behavior problems, were divided into two groups, above-average disabled readers ($N = 27$) and below-average disabled readers (N = 27). The above-average group had an average lag of 2 years in reading, while the below-average group had a lag of 4 years. The groups were matched on sex (only boys), age (mean, 13.0 years) and WISC-IQ (mean, 95). After the presentation of a series of symbols, the subject had to indicate via an answer card which figure, letter, or numeral he had seen first, which after that, and so on. The achievements of the below-average group were, on the whole, lower than those of the above-average group. But the stimuli used made a great deal of difference. *Only meaningful figures, letters, and numerals differentiated the two reading groups; the meaningless figures did not do so at all.*

There is a notable difference between meaningless and meaningful figures, letters, and numerals. Meaningless figures have, by defination, no name, while meaningful figures do, and letters and numerals are verbal in nature. When we are concerned with temporal series of stimuli that are verbal in nature or that have an inherent verbal label, the poorer readers are differentiated from better readers; when the recognition of a series of symbols depends primarily on nonverbal perceptual characteristics, the differences between the two reading groups disappear. This conclusion is reminiscent of that of Blank, Weider, and Bridger (1968).

A second experiment was also carried out with students of a school for children with learning and behavior problems (all boys; mean age, 12.0 years; mean WISC-IQ, 100). Above-average readers (N = 20) were retarded 2 years on the average, below-average readers (N = 20), 4 years. Both reading groups were matched on sex, age, and IQ. In each trial two different colored light flashes were presented one after the other, and the subject had to indicate which he had seen first or last. In comparison with the first experiment, presentation and interval time were greatly reduced: each flash continued for 100 msec, while the interval time was 75 msec. Because this experiment was concerned with verbally codifiable stimuli, it was expected that the above-average readers would obtain significantly better results than the below-average readers. This expectation proved to be correct. The above-average group had 71 percent correct answers, while the below-average group had 58 percent ($p < 0.05$). The relationship between temporal order perception and reading thus appears to be independent of the speed of presentation of the stimuli.

Above-average versus Below-average Normal Readers Another experiment used boys and girls from the first grade of an elementary school (mean age, 7.0 years; mean IQ, 110). Twelve above-average readers and 12 below-average readers were matched on sex, age, and IQ (Pintner, Cunningham, and Dursot*). The subjects were presented letters in succession. Each letter was shown for 1 second, and the interval between two presentations also lasted 1 second. The subjects were instructed to indicate the position of each letter in its series. The above-average readers performed significantly better than the below-average readers. *A positive correlation of 0.63 was found between memory for temporal order perception of letters and reading ability (0.58 after elimination of the IQ effect).*

In an investigation by Groenendaal and Bakker (1971) temporal sequences of meaningful and meaningless figures were presented to 7- and 10-year-old elementary school children. The subject had to indicate the temporal position of each figure in a series. Above-average readers achieved better results with meaningful figures than the below-average readers. This was especially true for 7-year-olds. With the meaningless figures, no differences were found between the two reading groups. The conclusions from this and the first experiment (Bakker, 1967a) are the same: *there is a temporal order perception-reading relationship for verbal or verbally codifiable stimuli.*

---

* References in languages other than English are omitted from the "Literature Cited" section and are marked with an asterisk in the text. Please write to the editors for a complete list of foreign-language references (the editors).

Temporal Order in Visual-Visual (TOVV) and Auditory-Visual (TOAV) Matching Temporal order perception apparently has predictive value with regard to reading ability. This conclusion is based on a study (Bakker, 1972a, 1972b) of a representative sample of 400 Dutch kindergarten children, ages 5 to 6. Two temporal order tests were administered. One test (TOVV) consisted of cards with meaningful figures presented in succession. Following the presentation of a series, the subject had to indicate which picture had been presented first and which afterwards. The second test (TOAV) consisted of an oral list of objects named successively by the investigator. As soon as the subject heard the words in a series, he was shown pictures of the objects named. He had to point out which object had been named first and which after that. *The scores of both temporal order tests administered in kindergarten correlated significantly and positively with reading scores in the first and second grades* (*r*-values between 0.30 and 0.43). TOAV predicted reading ability somewhat better than TOVV. Also, when the IQ effect was eliminated, the temporal order perception reading relationship remained.

TOAV was administered 1 and 2 years after the first presentation to the same children, who were now in elementary school. *At the ages of 6 and 7, girls were better at perceiving and remembering temporal sequences than boys; at the age of 8, however, this sex difference disappeared.* In view of the relationship between temporal order perception and reading, it seems that girls, on entering elementary school, are better equipped to learn to read than boys.

Another sex difference was ascertained in an investigation (Bakker 1970, 1972a) of 100 elementary school children. In this experiment letters were presented in temporal sequence, in visual, auditory, and haptic forms. The positions of the letters in a series had to be indicated. Girls of 7 and 8 years of age performed better than boys of this age group. By the ages of 9 to 11, no sex differences were found. The results of the experiments with both the kindergarten and the elementary school children point to a sex difference in the temporal perception of both verbal and verbally codifiable stimuli: *girls 5 to 8 years of age are more mature than boys of this age group.* Because temporal order perception relates to and even inheres in the reading process, one may expect that boys run more risks than girls in the process of learning to read in the first school years.

An implication of these findings is that dyslexic readers have more difficulty with temporal order tasks than do normal readers. An experiment (Bakker, 1972a) in which a number of normal and reading-disabled boys of 9 to 11 years of age were compared on their temporal ordering performance supported this hypothesis. The subjects were individually matched on age and WISC-IQ (mean, 103). The subjects were presented with visual, auditory, and haptic temporal sequences of letters. In each trial the subject indicated the order of succession of the letters in a series. In each of these sensory-input conditions, the normal boys achieved significantly better than the reading-disabled boys.

Temporal Order Perception (TOP) and Types of Reading Errors   Thus far, this discussion has dealt with only quantitative TOP-reading relationships: temporal order perception appears related to the number of correctly versus incorrectly read words in a reading test. The present authors were also interested in knowing whether there was a relationship between TOP and types of reading errors. Children from the first grade of a primary school were divided into above-average temporal order perceivers and below-average temporal order perceivers on the basis of scores on a test of temporal ordering using meaningful pictures. Each subject was given a selection to read. The reading errors were classified into 23 categories. Four of these categories concerned typical temporal ordering errors: changing of letter sequences (slot/stol, board/broad), putting words in the wrong sequence, reversing diphthongs (trein/trien, brain/brian), and anticipation of a following word (per trein/prein, by train/brain). This investigation (Bakker, 1970) showed that the below-average temporal order perceivers made significantly more errors in reading than the above-average temporal order perceivers, once again illustrating the TOP-reading relationship at the quantitative level. The extra errors in the below-average TOP group were almost all classifiable in the categoreis of typical temporal ordering errors named above. This illustrates the TOP-reading relationship at the qualitative level.

The experiments discussed led to the conclusion that there is a quantitatively and qualitatively specifiable relationship between temporal perception of verbal stimuli and reading ability. The relationship exists within the range of normal as well as disabled reading. *Temporal order perception in kindergarten predicts reading ability in elementary school.* It seems, therefore, that TOP conditions the reading process, and not vice versa.

CEREBRAL DOMINANCE AND READING DISABILITY

The concept of cerebral dominance is a bone of contention in reading disability research. Cerebral dominance is related to lateral dominance, a preference for one of the two halves of the body. It is a fascinating fact that there are two apparently identical brain halves; but, although the two halves appear to be anatomically similar, functionally this is not the case.

Functional asymmetry of the brain has, these past few years, been investigated with completely new techniques. An example of these new methods is the so-called dichotic listening equipment. In this method numerals or letters are presented to both ears at the same time. The left ear is presented with, for example, the letters b, k, and m, while c, l, and t are presented to the right ear in such a way that the subject hears b and c at the same time (b via the left and c via the right ear) and shortly after the pairs k—l and m—t. When the subject is asked to reproduce the letters he has heard, he usually remembers the letters heard via the right ear (left hemisphere) sooner and better than the other letters. On the other hand, if nonverbal sounds are presented, the achievements of the left ear are generally better than those of the right ear. These results point to the functional asymmetry of the brain: verbal functions are controlled primarily by the left hemisphere and nonverbal functions by the right hemisphere.

In the present authors' laboratory a monaural listening test is sometimes used to investigate ear asymmetry. In this technique the ears are stimulated at different times rather than at the same time, for example, first the right ear and then the left. Otherwise, the monaural procedure is the same as the dichotic one. It has been shown that ear asymmetry can be demonstrated by a monaural test as well as by the dichotic one. The question arises, is this asymmetry related to reading ability in general and reading disability in particular? The results of a number of studies seem to point to the presence of such a relationship.

A first investigation (Bakker, 1969) in the present authors' laboratory involved 50 right-handed girls from the fifth grade of an elementary school. They had a mean age of 10.5 years, a mean IQ of 117 (range, 82 to 146) and a reading ability corresponding to the population norm for that age group. The subjects were presented letters monaurally, and the letters had to be reproduced in the order of presentation. Thus, the temporal order perception of each ear was involved. The score obtained by the left ear was subtracted from that of the right. These between-ear differences were analyzed in relation to the reading scores. *The relationship between ear dominance and reading ability was found to be significant and positive.* The previous section described the relationship between temporal order perception and reading. This asymmetry investigation suggests that lateral differentiation of temporal perception is also related to reading.

De Haas investigated 40 dyslexic boys with a mean age of 11.5 years. They were divided into above-average and below-average readers. The subjects were given a dichotic listening test. The order of reproduction of what was heard was regarded as irrelevant (free recall). The above-average group showed significant right-ear (left-hemisphere) preference, while no ear asymmetry was found in the below-average group. The between-ear differences of the above-average readers were significantly larger than those of the below-average readers.

These two experiments, as well as other published investigations, had been conducted with older school children. Generally, proficient reading is connected with a right-ear preference and thus, one would assume, with left-hemispheric dominance for language. One can ask whether such a relationship is to be expected at younger school ages as well, because in the beginning school years the reading process differs from that at a later age. Smith (1971) has made it clear that the beginning reader focuses strongly on the text. He analyses the visual configuration before him, and on that basis he comes to understand the message contained in the text. The fluent reader, on the other hand, rapidly gathers an impression of the message the text bears; he does little other than test this impression on the visual configuration he sees. One of the main steps in early reading is perceptual analysis of, among other things, letter forms and sequences. These processes have become unconscious automatisms in fluent reading. Perception of spatial and temporal patterns is a nonverbal process and as such is apparently controlled by the nonverbal hemisphere (usually the right). Consideration of this participation of nonverbal perception in the early learning-to-read process led the present authors to predict that proficient reading in the early school years is paired with a bilateral representation of function, or possibly with a right hemispheric control of lingual and perceptual processes. Thus proficient early reading may go with lack of ear asymmetry or possibly with left-ear advantage.

The present authors' earlier studies tested the hypothesis that proficient early reading goes with absence of ear asymmetry (small absolute between-ear differences) and proficient advanced reading with presence of ear asymmetry (large absolute between-ear differences). This hypothesis was verified in four investigations (Bakker, Smink, and Reitsma, 1973). These experiments involved young (7 to 8 years of age) as well as older (9 to 11 years of age) elementary school children, and also young (9 to 10 years of age) and older (11 to 13 years of age) reading-disabled boys from schools for children with learning difficulties and behavior problems. The younger normal as well as the younger reading-disabled children were still in the early reading phase (the dyslexic children were, on the average, retarded 2 years in reading). Relatively high reading scores were paired with minimal ear differences in these children. The situation was the reverse for older normal and reading-disabled children: higher reading scores were obtained by children who had large ear differences. Figure 1, depicting the dominance-reading ability relationships in younger and older normal readers, illustrates these findings.

However, this series of experiments was not completely satisfactory because absolute between-ear differences (absolute value of left ear score minus right ear score) mask the effects of each ear separately. This problem was overcome in subsequent investigations (Bakker, Teunissen, and Bosch, 1976). A recent experiment in collaboration with Northern Illinois University most clearly evidenced developmental changes in the ear asymmetry reading pattern (Bakker, 1976). First-, second- and third-grade, normal right-handed boys and girls were presented monaural listening and standard reading tests. Asymmetric digit recall was analyzed in relation with reading proficiency in second and third graders. It was found that most

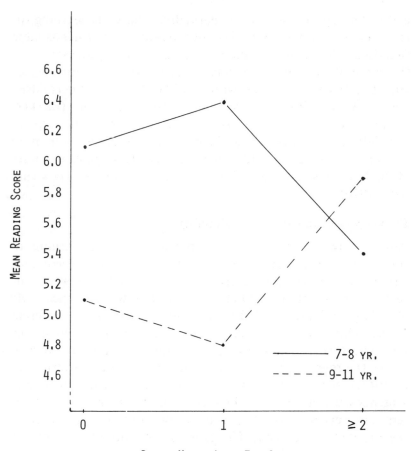

Figure 1. Relationship between ear dominance and reading ability in 7 to 8 and 9 to 11 year-old normal children. In the younger children, higher reading scores went with smaller ear differences. In the older children, the reverse was true. (Reprinted with permission from Bakker, Smink, and Reitsma, 1973.)

of the variance in the reading scores is accounted for by left ear performance in second graders and by right ear performance in third graders.

Considering the results of these experiments, one may conclude that the laterality-reading relationships at younger and older school ages differ markedly. The early learning-to-read process seems to be less dependent on left-hemisphere functioning than the advanced learning-to-read process. Thus, the cerebral mechanisms primarily subserving the learning-to-read process may change with age. However, some children may stay with right-hemisphere reading strategies (Bakker, Teunissen, and Bosch, 1976). Such stagnation would explain why left-ear advantage (right-hemisphere dominance) is more frequently found in older disabled readers than in older normal readers (Satz and Van Nostrand, 1972; Sparrow and Satz, 1970).

Picture Clues and Reading Disability

Attention processes play an important role in learning to read. The beginning reader is confronted with a complex visual pattern. He has to learn to discriminate between different letters, letter combinations, and letter sequences. He also has to learn that the same letters can have different forms. Thus, he must perceive the correct letter in spite of the different forms it can assume. In short, he must be able to derive the relevant information from the stimulus pattern. Not all information is relevant. The color of letters, words, and sentences has nothing to do with their meaning. Colored letters can support visual discrimination and perhaps increase the motivation to read. The latter is, no doubt, one of the purposes of the pictures that ornament most readers. The question needs to be asked, however, whether colors and pictures occasion negative as well as positive effects. In a number of experiments, Samuels (1967) has shown that, on the whole, pictures slow the learning-to-read process. It is especially the underachiever whose reading is hindered more than helped by illustrations. Samuels mentions the attention-distracting function of pictures as an important cause of this negative effect. The learner is inclined to name the pictures rather than to read the words.

The present authors conducted two experiments to study the effect of pictures on learning to read. The first investigation (Laman and Bakker*) involved reading-disabled boys with a mean age of 12 years and a mean WISC-IQ of 100. On the basis of their reading scores, they were divided into above-average and below-average readers. The groups did not differ in mean age and mean IQ. The subjects had to read a number of words in an unfamiliar script. Practice and test trials were given. The words to be read were printed on cards with or without a concrete illustration of the word. On the practice trials, half of the above-average and of the below-average group were presented words with a picture, the others without pictures. Each practice trial alternated with a test trial. On the test trial both groups were presented words without illustrations. The number of test trials necessary to reproduce the whole series of words twice without error was noted. Both the above-average and the below-average readers learned more slowly under the picture condition than under the no-picture condition. The negative effect of pictures was greatest, however, in the below-average group. The whole procedure was repeated with the same subjects 2 days later and again 4 weeks later. *Again, the readers who practiced with illustrations required more time to learn the words than those who practiced without illustrations.* Thus, this investigation supports Samuels' results. The present authors' samples were taken from a completely different population than his: the children were older and came from a different type of school. This increases the possibility of generalizing from the findings.

Effects of Simultaneously (SIM)
and Successively (SUC) Presented Pictures

The fact that illustrations are so widely used might mean that they have positive as well as negative effects. It occurred to the present authors that pictures can, among other things, serve as feedback. In a second experiment the present authors tried to keep the attention-distracting and the feedback-providing aspects separated. The subjects participating in the experiment were kindergarten children who could not yet read (mean age, 6.2 years). The children were given four words to learn to read as a pretest. These words were learned without illustrations. On the basis of the pretest scores, the subjects were matched in pairs and randomly divided between the simultaneous (SIM) and the successive (SUC) conditions. Then the subjects were given a new series of words to learn. In the SIM condition, the subjects practiced with pictures drawn on the *same side* of the card on which the words were printed. In the SUC condition, the pictures were on the *back* of the cards on which the words were printed. In the SIM condition, word and illustration were presented simultaneously. In the SUC condition, this presentation occurred successively: the subject read the word and then turned the card over to look at the picture. In a successive presentation, the subject is first obliged to give all his attention to the word and then he can use the picture to verify his response.

In the experiment, practice trials were alternated with test trials. During the test trials, reading occurred without illustrations. The number of trials required to read the series of words without errors twice in succession was noted. The number of pretest trials minus the number of test trials was the criterion for the effect of practice in the SIM and the SUC conditions. The four pretest words were randomly chosen from a pool of eight words; the remaining words were used for the practice and test trials. Practice in the simultaneous condition had a significant negative effect on the learning process. Neither a positive nor a negative effect could be established for practice in the successive condition.

A rather interesting finding concerning the results in the SUC condition might be mentioned. After subjects who practiced in the SUC condition were split on the basis of their pretest scores into above-average and below-average readers, a significant negative influence of successive presentation was found in the above-average readers and a significant positive influence in the below-average readers. The SIM condition did not have this differential effect. The conclusion is, therefore, that *illustrations presented simultaneously with words have a negative effect on both good and poor readers*. The successive presentation of words and pictures may have a negative effect on good readers but a positive effect on poor readers. This needs to be reconfirmed.

CONCLUSION

The problem of reading disability can be approached in various ways. This is so because of the complexity of the learning-to-read process. The present authors' investigations represent only a small sample of the many approaches. The need has arisen for dyslexia models that include as many reading-related factors as possible. A neuropsychological model was recently developed by Satz and Sparrow (1970). Their theory presumes a functional immaturity of the whole left hemisphere in children suffering from specific developmental dyslexia. Such a cortical condition would predict low performance of functions that are controlled primarily by the left hemisphere. Some of these functions have been discussed in this chapter. The perception of successively presented verbal stimuli (left hemisphere) was shown to be disturbed in disabled readers, while this was not found for the successive perception of nonverbal (right hemisphere) stimuli. Both temporal order perception of verbal stimuli and reading are most likely under the control of the left hemisphere in older school children, as is the auditory perception of digits, which, in other experiments, was shown to correlate with reading achievements.

The results of the present authors' investigations suggest that the functional maturity of the right hemisphere may be of importance to the early stages of the learning-to-read process. It is felt, therefore, that Satz and Sparrow's model should be extended because it stresses the importance of only left hemispheric maturity to all modes of reading.

Although researchers all want their work, sooner or later, to benefit the dyslexic child, there is a gap between etiology and therapy. Training some of the functions underlying reading ability does not necessarily lead to an improvement of that ability. Colthof* found that training temporal order perception, for instance, scarcely affected the reading level of dyslexic boys. On the other hand, a program of systematic training in the reading process itself was more successful (Evers-Emden*). For the time being, nobody knows precisely all the factors affecting the learning-to-read process nor how these factors interact. As long as this situation exists, programs of a broad spectrum are preferred along with the more direct therapeutic approaches to reading.

LITERATURE CITED

Bakker, D. J. 1966. Sensory dominance in normal and backward readers. Percept. Mot. Skills 23:1055.

Bakker, D. J. 1967a. Temporal order, meaningfulness, and reading ability. Percept. Mot. Skills 24:1027.

Bakker, D. J. 1967b. Sensory dominance and reading ability. J. Commun. Disord. 1:316.

Bakker, D. J. 1969. Ear asymmetry with monaural stimulation: Task influences. Cortex 5:36.

Bakker, D. J. 1970. Temporal order perception and reading retardation. In: D. J. Bakker and P. Satz (eds.), Specific Reading Disability; Advances in Theory and Method, pp. 81–96. Rotterdam University Press, Rotterdam.

Bakker, D. J. 1972a. Temporal Order in Disturbed Reading; Developmental and Neuropsychological Aspects in Normal and Reading Retarded Children. Rotterdam University Press, Rotterdam.

Bakker, D. J. 1972b. Reading disability and the perception of temporal order. Address to the Tenth Annual Academy of Aphasia Meeting, Rochester, New York.

Bakker, D. J. 1976. Perceptual Asymmetries and Reading Proficiency. Research Report nr. 1976-2. Paedologisch Instituut, Amsterdam.
Bakker, D. J., Smink, T., and Reitsma, P. 1973. Ear dominance and reading ability. Cortex 9.
Bakker, D. J., Teunissen, J., and Bosch, J. 1976. Development of laterality—reading patterns. In: R. M. Knights and D. J. Bakker (eds.), The Neuropsychology of Learning Disorders: Theoretical Approaches, pp. 207–220. University Park Press, Baltimore.
Birch, H. G. 1962. Dyslexia and the maturation of visual function. In: J. Money (ed.), Reading Disability, pp. 161–169. Johns Hopkins Press, Baltimore.
Birch, H. G., and Belmont, L. 1964. Auditory-visual integration in normal and retarded readers. Am. J. Orthopsych. 34:852.
Birch, H. G., and Belmont, L. 1965. Auditory-visual integration, intelligence and reading ability in school children. Percept. Mot. Skills 20:295.
Birch, H. G., and Belmont, L. 1966. Development and disturbance in auditory-visual integration. EENT Digest 28:47.
Blank, M., and Bridger, W. H. 1966. Deficiencies in verbal labeling in retarded readers. Am. J. Orthopsych. 36:840.
Blank, M., Weider, S., and Bridger, W. H. 1968. Verbal deficiencies in abstract thinking in early reading retardation. Am. J. Orthopsych. 38:823.
Groenendaal, H. A., and Bakker, D. J. 1971. The part played by mediation processes in the retention of temporal sequences by two reading groups. Hum. Dev. 14:62.
Karp, E., and Birch, H. G. 1969. Hemispheric differences in reaction time to verbal and non-verbal stimuli. Percept. Mot. Skills 29:475.
Lovell, K. and Gorton, A. 1968. A study of some differences between backward and normal readers of average intelligence. Br. J. Educ. Psych. 38:240.
Rudnick, M., Sterritt, G. M., and Flax, M. 1967. Auditory and visual rhythm perception and reading ability. Child Dev. 38:581.
Samuels, S. J. 1967. Attentional process in reading: The effect of pictures on the acquisition of reading responses. J. Educ. Psych. 58:337.

Satz, P., and Sparrow, S. S. 1970. Specific developmental dyslexia: A theoretical formulation. In: D. J. Bakker and P. Satz (eds.), Specific Reading Disability: Advances in Theory and Method, pp. 17–40. Rotterdam University Press, Rotterdam.

Satz, P., and Van Nostrand, K. 1972. Developmental dyslexia: An evaluation of a theory. In: P. Satz and J. J. Ross (eds.), The Disabled Learner: Early Detection and Intervention, pp. 121–148. Rotterdam University Press, Rotterdam.

Sparrow, S. S., and Satz, P. 1970. Dyslexia, laterality and neuropsychological development. In: D. J. Bakker and P. Satz (eds.), Specific Reading Disability: Advances in Theory and Method, pp. 41–60. Rotterdam University Press, Rotterdam.

Smith, F. 1971. Understanding Reading: A Psycholinguistic Analysis of Reading and Learning to Read. Holt, Rinehart and Winston, New York.

Index

Multisensory learning, 19, 161

Neural Efficiency Analyzer
(NEA), 83
Neurological and neuro-
psychological findings,
relationship between, 125
Neurological examination
findings, 126
Neurological examinations
versus neuropsychological
findings, difference in
evaluative strategies of,
125
Neurological learning
disabilities, causes of, 6
Neurological screening test
cutting scores, problems
involved in, 120
Neurons, 112
Neurophysiological deficit in
disabled readers, 86
Neuropsychological deficits and
strengths, and the
teaching approach, 130
Neurophysiological-type
measures, in conjunction
with psychoeducational
tests, 78
Neuropsychological and
neurological findings,
relationship between, 125
Neuropsychological assessment,
use of special tests in,
123
Neuropsychological findings,
126

versus neurological
examinations, 125
difference in evaluative
strategies of, 125
Neuropsychological interpretive
approach to treatment,
144
Neuropsychological test battery,
123, 124
Neuropsychological test profiles,
illustrative cases of,
131–143

Occipital lobe, 7, 60
Occipital lobe dysfunction, 33
Occipital region of subordinate
hemisphere, lesions in, 33
Occipitoparietal regions,
bilateral lesions of, 35
Optic agnosia. *See* Visual
agnosia
Oral command, as instigator but
not regulator of action,
53
Oral instruction, assumption of
controlling function of,
52
Orally conditioned motor
reaction, 53
"Orienting reaction," 102
"Overloaded" children, 7
Overt speech, first manifestations of, as "highest
regulator of human
behavior," 55

Pacific Medical Center, 3